The
TWELVE
GREATEST
GIFTS We Give
Our Children

How to Be the Mom Your Children Truly Need
and Create the Family You Always Wanted

TRUDI MITCHELL BARTOW

Mom, Educator, Certified Professional Life Coach

ISBN: 978-1-4834-4735-3 (sc)
ISBN: 978-1-4834-4734-6 (e)

Library of Congress Control Number: 2016903035

Because of the dynamic nature of the Internet, any web addresses or links contained in this book may have changed since publication and may no longer be valid. The views expressed in this work are solely those of the author and do not necessarily reflect the views of the publisher, and the publisher hereby disclaims any responsibility for them.

Any people depicted in stock imagery provided by Thinkstock are models, and such images are being used for illustrative purposes only. Certain stock imagery © Thinkstock.

Lulu Publishing Services rev. date: 3/28/2016

To my children, Meghan, Matthew, and Mary Kate. Thank you for giving me my greatest role in life as your mother. Nothing else I ever do will mean as much or bring me more joy. My greatest reward is watching you live your dreams.

You are the reason this book was written, you are the examples throughout this book, and your encouragement to put everything to paper is what made this a reality. I love you each more than you could ever imagine.

Acknowledgments

Special thanks to

- My husband, John, for always valuing my importance to our children, for trusting my vision for how best to raise them, and for being my partner through life. Our family began when I married you.

- My parents, Jim and Gwyn, for raising me to understand the importance of hard work, honesty, respect, and determination.

- My angel mom, Garnie, for giving me life, raising me with love for our few years together, and guiding me from heaven.

- My grandparents, Hazel and Lonnie, for believing in my purpose from the very beginning.

- And of course, Ann McIndoo, my author's coach, who got this book out of my head and into my hands.

Contents

Introduction

This book has been a lifetime in the making, from the time I was a little girl born in the 1960s to now. My experiences as a child, as a mother, and as an educator have shaped my views about motherhood. From an early age, I knew how important motherhood was. I tragically lost my own mother when I was three years old, and that impacted me in such a profound way. From that point onward, I needed to mother, and anyone could be a target for my mothering and nurturing instinct—my younger sister, neighborhood children, children I babysat for, family members, even friends. I knew that it was going to be my life's work to be a mom.

As I grew up, I always thought about that future mother part of me, even though I encountered difficult situations along the way. Family relationships and disagreements created a lot of turmoil, but I never lost my desire and need to be a mom. Sometimes, I would say to myself when I was experiencing difficulties, "When I grow up, I do not want my kids to ever experience this or feel like this." I knew there was another way, and I was determined to create it for my kids.

That was part of who I was growing up, and everyone knew I was destined to be a mother. My parents were very aware of that mothering instinct in me from an early age. When I did marry young and fifteen months later found out I was expecting my first child, my dad said to me, "You won't need those dolls to mother anymore. You will have that child you always wanted."

As much as I had dreamed about it, nothing could have prepared me for how life-altering the reality of motherhood would be. I was blessed with this child that God had given me. I was responsible for this child, and yet nothing told me what to do or where to focus my energy so that I could raise my child to be a good individual, a contributing member of society, and a compassionate soul with a loving heart.

I never expected my child to be perfect, because no human is, but I wanted to do my best to mold my child into a good person who would be a positive energy in the world. As I was mothering that first child, then the second, and then the third, I was thinking about the kind of people I wanted them to be, the situations I had experienced as a child that I wanted to protect them from, and the actions I could take to raise them in an atmosphere of love and acceptance. These, after all, were the children whom I loved and adored above all things.

It was trial and error in those early years, thinking about those things and reading as much as I could but not really finding the information I wanted to find. No child comes with a manual on how to be a mom, and I realized that very quickly. Before I took home my first baby from the hospital, the nurse came in to teach me things such as how to suction her nose, how to nurse, how much she should be sleeping, and when to make her first doctor's appointment. The nurse said nothing that was going to impact how I needed to raise her (nor did anyone else, for that matter).

After going through my children's toddlerhood, their preteen years, their teenage years that took so much time and energy, and on to their adulthood, I heard from my own kids, "Mom, when you were raising us and you had rules about who we could hang out with, I never understood it. Now I do." "Thanks, Mom, for teaching us to be responsible." "When I have kids, I am going to raise them the way you raised us!"

I realized, even though my kids were adults, they were recognizing and appreciating the way that I had raised them.

As my children grew, people would ask me how I got my kids to be so close or how I got my kids to love education or how I got my kids to be responsible or goal oriented. I would think, *Well, how* did *I do that?*

When my youngest child was in elementary school, I went back to work after being a stay-at-home mom since my first was born. As an educator, I saw the other side of what happens when children are not taught certain things at home. It was a culmination of all of these things that made me realize I had a message I needed to share. Then my children, Meghan, Matthew, and Mary Kate, began to tell me, "Mom, you should just write a book."

The purpose behind this book is to help moms realize that we are all in this together. As moms, we just do the best that we can. We are not perfect and will not always make the right decisions. In fact, we will not always do the right things. But if we are consistent and if we recognize the importance of our role as moms, we can change the world through the children we raise.

No one else can be our children's mother. No one else will love them like we do. No one else can have a greater impact on the people they grow to be.

What happens after they become adults, we have no control over. We have the chance to impact their lives as we are raising them. We can guide them to follow the path that we hope they will choose, the path that will make God smile and see that they are trying to do the right things in their lives.

Raising children is a learning experience. It is not about being the perfect mom. Our kids do not need us to be the perfect mom. What they need is a committed mom who treasures her role, who treasures her children as the blessings that they are in her life and recognizes that she has a vital role to play. God gave us the gift of our children for a reason. We have to do the very best that we can in raising them.

We owe it to our children to make them our priority and give them the gifts that will change their lives, the lives of their children, and the world in the process. Our children might beg for a pony, a puppy, or a new bike, thinking that happiness would be theirs if they just had that gift. What our children really need are gifts that transcend something they can simply possess. The greatest gifts we give our children are the gifts that make us the moms they truly need and that create for us the family we always wanted.

Chapter One
The Gift of Unconditional Love

*You must first teach a child he is loved; only
then is he ready to learn everything else.*
—Unknown

Putting It into Practice

You might be thinking as you read this, *Of course my
children need unconditional love. That is what moms are
supposed to give their children.* Most moms accept this easily
in theory, but when they have to put it into practice, it can
be difficult. When you wholeheartedly love your children and
accept them for who they are, you unconditionally love your
children.

To your children, you are everything. They look to you for
everything they have, for all their needs to be met, especially
in those early years. In essence, you are their world. Since they
are looking to you, you have to show them you are going to love
them unconditionally, just as God loves them unconditionally.
Since they are looking to you to show them their worth, you
have to show them that they are valued, they are treasured,
and you feel blessed that you are their mom and get to love and
raise them every day.

They are looking to you for that unconditional love, and you have to give it to them. Your children are the future, and they must be secure in themselves and love themselves in order to love others. All you have to do is look at the headlines today— whether the stories are about people leading our country, people leading corporations, or just people down the street who make wrong choices and put themselves and others in danger—to see that children must be raised with values and love.

Since your kids are looking to you and you are going to be the one to instill those values in them from early on, you have to love them unconditionally from the beginning. That will set the foundation for everything. They must be secure in that love of themselves in order to be able to love others. You will not be constantly looking for things they are doing wrong. You will not be picking them apart for one reason or another.

That does not mean you will not discipline them. It does mean you will love them for who they are, and they have to know that they are loved for who they are. That love is not based on how good they are today or whether they did what you asked them to do today. You will love them no matter what.

Before your children are born, you have a vision, one that often forms from the first moment you discover you are having a baby. *When this child is born*, you think, and you follow with thoughts of what your child will be like and what you are going to do for him or her. Your thoughts might be of the life you want your child to have and your hopes of what he or she will become, but those visions are not reality. Those visions may not come to fruition. Maybe your child will be a different sex from what you anticipated, or his or her personality may be different from what you envisioned. For the love of your child, you must adjust what you thought and live in the reality of who your child is.

Accept the reality of the children you are blessed with. Wholeheartedly love and accept those children. Remember that your children are not clones of you; this is not a chance for everything you wish had been different for you to be corrected in them. Your children are not going to do things as you would do; they will not be who you are.

You will still have hopes and dreams for your children. Of course you will. Embrace the fact that each of your children is his or her own individual, his or her own person, and help each one of them grow into the best version of who he or she is.

Think, too, that God has entrusted your children's souls to you. Love your children wholeheartedly without conditions. God has given you these blessings, these souls to nurture and to raise, and it is your responsibility to do that, loving them unconditionally as you go.

What Does It Mean?

For there to be unconditional love, your children must recognize that they have it. You may think you love your children unconditionally, but do they know that? For it to truly be unconditional love, your children have to feel it from you, know it is there, and recognize it as unconditional. They have to feel that no matter what is going on, no matter what trials or tribulations or bad days you have had, your unconditional love for them is never in doubt. *Mom may be having a rough day, and she may be in a bad mood, but I never doubt that she loves me.*

Your children must feel like they are loved without conditions, not because they have done something good and not because they are doing something that you want them to do. It has to be love without reasons, love without actions or behaviors factored in. It must be love with no conditions; love in its purest form is unconditional love.

Children must be loved for their unique traits and personalities. Each of your children will have his or her own unique personality and set of traits, and you must find the value in those so that you can love your children unconditionally.

3

Recognize, especially if you have multiple children, that each child will not have the same traits and personality. Think about the interests, personality, and talents your child has, and accept that these do not have to be the same as yours. This is your opportunity to find new ways to be interested in new things, through your children.

When my son, Matthew, first wanted to play lacrosse in middle school, I knew nothing about the game except that it involved a stick, a ball, and players running across a field, similar to soccer. We had recently moved to New England, and his new friends were playing lacrosse. Even when not on the field, these boys had sticks in hand, constantly trying to catch and keep the ball in the pocket on the end of their sticks.

After agreeing to let Matthew play lacrosse, we registered him for a local league and purchased the necessary uniform and equipment. The first time he got dressed for a game and came out of his room, he was padded to what seemed like twice his size. I thought, *What in the world am I allowing him to do if he has to be padded up like this even to get on the field?*

Matthew loved playing lacrosse, and despite my early fears for his safety, lacrosse became a favorite family pastime. We all would head to the field on game day to watch Matthew play. Over the years, we learned the ins and outs of the game, and I was always the loudest cheerleader from the sidelines. That never would have happened without my son.

Think about your own children. What are their interests? What are their personality traits? What are their talents that will allow you a chance to experience something new through them? Their interests will not necessarily be tied to something you enjoy or have done before. By getting to the heart of their interests, personality traits, and talents, you will show that you love them unconditionally because you will learn to appreciate them and show that appreciation by taking an interest in the things important to them.

Getting Past the Preconceived Vision

As I mentioned earlier, you might dream about your child from the time you first find out you are having a baby. All the way through those sleepless nights, you are thinking and dreaming about all the things this child can accomplish and all the hopes and dreams you have for him. Still, be always mindful that your children are not here to complete unfulfilled dreams you may have.

You may have a child who wants to try an activity that interested you when you were younger but that you were never able to pursue. As you encourage her to try that activity, be careful not to place a burden on her to be something you couldn't be. If you never got to be a dancer, don't force her to be that dancer. If you always wanted to play piano, but your child is not interested in learning to play, respect that. You can encourage him to experience something, and maybe it will be something he enjoys or excels at. However, if he chooses not to take part in an activity you are encouraging, or if he tries it and finds that it is not of interest to him, then you must allow him to make those choices.

Why is it important to let your children be their own people? You are raising children to eventually be contributing members of society; you want them to be good people and make a difference in the world. With all of those things in mind, you have to let them be their own people because it is the gift that they bring to the world that will make the difference. You must let them be who they are and love who they are. Give your children the strength of knowing that they are valued for the people they are.

When I was growing up, I excelled at school. I needed to be good at school; it helped to fill a void. I was a rule follower. I did all the things I was supposed to do, and I did not rock the boat. I felt comfortable excelling at school; it gave me a sense of purpose. I got straight As, joined clubs, served as a school leader, and danced on the drill team. I never struggled through school; there was never a subject that I had major difficulty with.

With my oldest daughter, Meghan, it was difficult for me to recognize at first the struggle she was having with math because I had never experienced that difficulty. She was in honors math, but she would be in tears as she was completing homework. As her struggle continued and the stress began to take its toll, we talked about the best move to make.

I had to come to the realization that this was a struggle for her. I had to help her and provide what she needed to get past the struggle so that she could be successful. However, I had to back off in the sense that this was difficult for her, and I couldn't expect that she would excel at the subject. Meghan was not born with the same set of strengths and weaknesses that I had. As her mom, I had to help her through the difficulty, and I had to accept that just because I didn't struggle with math didn't mean she would not struggle.

Then this rule follower, this motivated student who had always gotten good grades, had a bright son who breezed through school. In the earlier years, I had a bit more control, and I could make sure Matthew was following through on what was expected of him at school. By the time he got to high school, he was recognizing that he did not have to work very hard to get good grades, and he chose to sit back, thinking that missing a few homework assignments or not studying for tests didn't matter that much.

His favorite teacher recognized the symptom right away and told Matthew, "You know, I figured out what it is with you. You have LAD."

"LAD?" my son asked.

"Yes, lazy ass disorder."

Matthew thought that was funny because here was a teacher whom he respected, calling him out on the fact that he had what he needed to be successful yet was choosing not to do his homework assignment. That was laziness because he had the ability to do better. As someone who had been a rule follower and gotten good grades in school, I couldn't imagine that my bright son would choose not to reach his fullest potential. I had to discipline him and impose on him the importance of completing and turning in his homework. He could not be lazy and choose not to put forth his best effort.

Unconditional love is all about recognizing that your children are individuals and that they will do things differently than you may want them to do. It is your role as their mom to guide them through those choices and help them be the best they can be. Unconditional love is about accepting their individuality, building on their strengths, and helping them overcome weaknesses.

Growing up, I was also a girlie girl. Many people thought of me as the girl who hated getting in the mud, didn't like camping, hated outdoorsy activities, and did not like the sun, although I did do those things if required. Those activities just were not my favorite things.

When my youngest child, Mary Kate, came along, she was the opposite. She loved to play with cars, she loved to build things, and she even loved to pick up bugs. She was a regular handy-girl. When she was in high school, my husband and I were sitting downstairs, and she said, "Don't come upstairs, and do not come in my room."

We heard banging and moving and wondered what in the world was going on. After a period of time, she called us upstairs to see what she had been doing. She had completely taken apart her bed, screws and all, every single piece, and moved it aside because she wanted her bed to sit back in the alcove of her bedroom, and it would fit only if the mattress and box spring were on the floor. Since it could not fit there with the headboard and footboard, she had removed them and moved all those pieces of the bed as well as the mattress and box spring. She had the tools and the know-how to do it. This was not something that I ever would have done.

As I was raising my kids, every time they showed their individuality, the traits that were different from mine, it was a chance to appreciate the unique individuals I was raising. It was a chance to see life from the other side. I was able to experience life through their eyes and fully appreciate all of their unique traits and personalities.

Growing up, I loved, loved, loved to read. I had a lot of books as a child, and my first two children were very much the same. They loved books and reading, and it was a love that we shared. I delighted in the fact that they would choose a book over a doll or a book over a game. I would think, *Look how much they love books! Just like I love books.*

When Mary Kate came along, things were different. Books were not her first choice of activity. Still, I would read to her just like I read with Meghan and Matthew, even though it was not her favorite activity. She was not going to choose a book if there were cars, bugs, or experiments waiting to be created.

With multiple children, it was interesting to see that each one was his or her own individual. I could not expect them to be the same, nor would I have wanted that. Each individual child is loved unconditionally for the person he or she is.

Express Unconditional Love with Words

Express your love for your children with words. For some moms, this is an easy thing to do. You may be one of those moms who is always telling your kids that you love them and value them. For some people, however, saying those words does not come easily. If you are one of those who find it difficult to say the words "I love you," you can use other words to express love to your children while you are working to become more comfortable with "I love you." For example, you might say, "You made me so happy today when you gave me a kiss before you went to school." This way, you show them love by expressing through words something that you appreciate about them. You might say how much you love their cuddles, how much you love spending time with them, or how much you love reading with them. These are all ways of expressing your love for them through words.

The words "I love you" mean something special to your child. Every child deserves to hear those words and needs to hear those words. Make it a priority to say "I love you" in addition to finding other ways to express your love.

When I grew up, I heard the words "I love you" often from my parents, my grandparents, and my aunts and uncles; we were people who vocalized "I love you." When we had a tragedy or experienced difficult times, knowing that I was loved and hearing that through words really helped me cope with the difficulties and heartbreaks. On the other hand, my husband was raised in a family where they did not frequently say those words, and it took the loss of his father for the family to recognize the need to express their love more frequently. Now not a phone call or visit ends without an "I love you."

If you are struggling with "I love you," start slowly. Maybe say an "I love you" at the end of the day, before you go to work or school, or at the end of a conversation. However you work it in, get into the habit so that at least once a day, your children are hearing those words "I love you."

When you are praising or disciplining your children, tell them you love them. Especially when disciplining your children, find ways to work in the "I love you." This is a time when children can easily feel your disappointment, so reassuring them of your love helps them accept that they are being disciplined *because* you love them. Your children need to hear why you are disciplining them, but they also need to know that you still love them. Use the words "I love you" when you are praising your children as well. "I am so happy that you took the time to make a drawing for me. I love it, and I love you!"

As your children get older and start calling you on the phone, say "I love you" at the end of those phone conversations. With teens and older children, phone conversations become less frequent because the main mode of communication seems to be texting or instant messaging. Still, an "I love you" is the perfect way to wrap up even those conversations.

Those three heartfelt words should be words your children hear on a regular basis. They are not, however, the only way to express love. The foundation should be that your child is hearing "I love you" at least once a day, but you can also find other ways to express that love. Sentiments such as "I thank God for you," "I am proud of you," "you make me smile," and any loving affirmation lets your children know they have a special place in your heart.

Make these affirmations an integral part of your interactions with your children. Don't save them only for special occasions. Your child is a gift from God, so every day is a special occasion. If when you are praising your children, disciplining your children, and sharing special time with your children, you voice and express your love through words, you will build a solid foundation of love and acceptance. Expressing love through words should be a regular part of your interactions.

When expressing love, be sincere. Your children recognize a perfunctory "I love you" and know if there is no meaning behind it. Say the words so that your child can feel the emotion and heartfelt meaning behind those words.

When my children were little, I used what I call "the power of the napkin." Every morning when I made their lunches, I would write notes on the napkins that I tucked in their lunchboxes. "Good luck on your math test today," a note might say, or "I am saying a prayer for you." "I am sending you a hug." "Take a deep breath and know you are loved, even if Susie is still mad at you." "I am excited to see your performance tonight."

Whatever I thought they might need to hear that day, that is the message I would write. Whatever challenges, fears, joys, or hopes they were experiencing, I could use the napkin to let them know they were not alone. It could be about anything that was going on in their life. I would write a short message and sign it:

I love you,
Mom

When I first started doing this, it surprised my children. "Mom, there was a note in my lunchbox!" I continued to do this every time I made their lunches, even through middle school and into high school (although the frequency of taking a lunch began to dwindle). Even when they were old enough to make their own lunches, I would write a napkin note and sneak it in their lunchboxes when the boxes sat on the counter or in the refrigerator.

When Matthew was in middle school, I began finding those napkin notes tucked in his pocket when I checked pockets before doing laundry. It would make me smile as I thought about him reading the note, experiencing a moment of happiness, and then, rather than throwing the napkin away with his lunch trash, choosing to stick it in his pocket. Maybe he stuck it there so his friends wouldn't see it, but I believe this was his way of carrying that loving thought with him all day. Finding that napkin note tucked in his pocket always brought a smile to my face—even if I was just sorting laundry.

Express Love through Actions

In addition to expressing love with words, you must also express your love with actions. Words alone are not enough. You can say until you are blue in the face that you love them, and you can say words of appreciation and that you thank God for them all of the time, but without actions, something is going to be missing. Expressions of love through actions are an integral part of raising children and helping them to recognize that they are loved unconditionally.

You can do many things with your children that will help them recognize your unconditional love. Take time to have conversations with your children; find out what they are thinking, feeling, and wondering. Push them on the swing, make arts and crafts with them, read them a story, and cuddle with them on the sofa. Be their biggest cheerleader, their biggest supporter.

Throughout each day, find opportunities to spend time with your child and express through actions your unconditional love. Find things that you enjoy doing together and do those things. Share that time together. In your busy life raising children, you might think that you do not have one more moment to spare or one more ounce of energy to spare, but your children need you to find that time and energy.

When you take the time to express love with actions, it sends a very powerful message to your child. Since your focus is on expressing unconditional love through actions, these actions should not have conditions. They should be heartfelt interactions, should be truly from a place of love, and should not be contingent on the child's behavior. If you say to your child, "If you clean your room, then we will do some arts and crafts together," that is conditional. If you say, "If you clean off the table and stack the dishes, then we will play basketball," that is conditional. Whether the proposed interaction is reading a book or playing outside on the swing, if your child must complete an action to get time with you, your child will see the condition. Instead find moments where you can say, "Hey, let's sit down and read a book together," or "I've missed you today; let's go outside and garden together."

If your child likes to take walks with you, set aside time to do that. If your son likes to play basketball, shoot some hoops in the driveway before dinner. If your daughter wants you to play dolls with her, find time to do that. You know what your

12

children like to do and what will mean the most to them. These are all ways to express actions of unconditional love.

The absolute perfect time to share and express unconditional love through actions is at bedtime. When my daughter Meghan was born, I started the bedtime ritual as soon as she was on a schedule. As additional children arrived, they too had their own bedtime rituals. In those early years, the bedtime rituals would begin with baths, pajamas, and brushing teeth. I would snuggle up close with each one of them on their own beds and read a few bedtime stories to them, and as they got older and could read, I made sure that they had time to read out loud to me.

After we spent time reading, I would take the time to tuck them in. I mean literally tuck them into bed: let them snuggle down into the bed and get all comfortable and then tuck the sheet and blanket around them. They felt safe, secure, and at home in their beds and felt that mommy-love as they ended their day. After tucking them in, I would ask them what I call "the daily question." I asked each one as I tucked him or her into bed, "What was the best thing that happened to you today?"

I would watch with a smile on my face as they really thought about the question and how they wanted to answer. By asking what the best thing was, I could find out what the big highlight of their day had been, what event had really made a positive impression on them. I also wanted them to realize that even on their worst day, there was something they could be grateful for.

Take the time daily to talk to your children as you tuck them into bed. For me, that was such precious time that even if I was out in the evening for a meeting or some other activity and my husband had to put our children to bed, as soon as I got home, I would check to see if they were still awake. If so, I would quietly go into the children's rooms and give them a kiss, tuck them in, and ask the daily question. Even when they had grown up and did not need me to read to them anymore or listen to them read, I still did the tucking in, always giving them a kiss good-night and letting them know that I loved them by taking the time to find out what was important about their day.

The dinner table is another opportunity for precious time together. Gathering around the family dinner table for a meal together expresses love through actions. Even when you are busy, when the family grows, when everyone has activities, and when it becomes harder to get everyone together, keep that dinner table ritual as many nights as you can. Make every effort to prioritize that time because that is when you really have a chance for the family to come together, listen, talk, share, and appreciate the bond of family. Your children can share about their day—the good and bad—and then receive the input and support of parents and siblings. You are bonding as those day-to-day happenings in each other's lives are shared at the dinner table. Make sure you have that time together.

As my kids got older and became teenagers, I had to work hard to keep the dinner table as part of our routine. My husband loved to eat in front of the television if he could get away with it. Some nights, everyone would start getting their plates ready, thinking they were going to inch their way into the family room, sit in front of the television, and watch TV as they ate. I would say, "Television is off. We are sitting together at the table as a family for dinner."

Some of them would roll their eyes, saying, "But, Mom …" But I remained firm, reiterating that we were sitting at the table for dinner. I knew this routine had value, and I was not going to relinquish that time. In the moment, they might have preferred to be watching TV as they ate, but they can't wait to have meals together when they are all home now. Those times together as a family were priceless. Support, love, and appreciation were exchanged around our dinner table, and that was far more important than a show on television. As a mom and as a family, bond with your children at the dinner table every night that you can.

Embrace Unique Personalities

Each child has his or her own unique personality, and you must embrace those unique personalities and love your children unconditionally for those personalities. Your children are special just as they are, for who they are. You must make them understand this. You do not expect them to be like you or their siblings or anybody else. You love them for who they are.

Think about your children and those traits that are unique about them and that you love about them. Even if a child has personality traits that are not the same as yours or are difficult personality traits, you can still find value in those traits and how they will serve your child well as he or she grows into an adult. Focus on the positives in those traits, and love and appreciate them in your child.

When I was raising my children, I had to recognize this myself. My first two children were pretty mellow babies and pretty mellow children; discipline was easy. Very often I could just look at Meghan and Matthew the wrong way, and that was enough to get them back in line. Sometimes a few stern words were necessary to take care of a situation, but much more than that was not usually required.

When my third child was born, she was very different. Mary Kate pushed my buttons and tested my limits. She had a personality very different from my own. It was not uncommon to find her painting all over the floor, making concoctions all over the kitchen, or throwing a tantrum when things did not go her way. She just had a more intense personality, but there was never a moment that I did not love her.

I reminded myself to look at those traits in a positive way. I had to learn to appreciate the creativity, the originality, the intensity. Even though those traits made parenting more difficult, I thought of this as a chance to improve my parenting skills. I tell her even to this day that she tested my parenting skills. God must have thought that I needed that—to be tested a little bit. I would tell myself and others that her spunk would serve her well as an adult, that creativity was going to help her find her passion, and that originality was going to allow her to grow into her own person.

Once while we were visiting my parents, when Mary Kate was about four, my little one put her shoes on the wrong feet. My mother mentioned to her that she had her shoes on the wrong feet, and Mary Kate replied, "I know that, Grammy. I like to wear them that way." That was my youngest daughter, and that was her personality. She marched to the beat of a different drummer. That was okay, and I very much loved her for that.

Even though my little one could be difficult, she tested my parenting skills in a way that I never expected they would be tested, and she made me a better parent in the long run. She was in my life for a reason, and I loved her unconditionally. I recognized there was value in my child even though she was different than I was. We formed a very tight bond because of that, and we are still close today.

Love your children's uniqueness even when it conflicts with your own personality. It may be a little more difficult to manage sometimes, but love your children in spite of those difficulties, in spite of those personality traits that are different from your own. Your children are going to know that they are loved. They will feel cherished because they are loved even though you have those differences.

When I think about my own personality traits compared to my three children's personalities, there are differences, of course. Growing up, I was a social butterfly. Two of my children love to be social, out with large groups of friends, attending parties, enjoying the company of many. Another enjoys quiet evenings at home, spending time with her best friend, or meeting a small group for dinner. I tended to be stylish; I liked to be trendy and put-together. One daughter is trendy, one prefers comfort, and neither likes lipstick as much as I do. My son, on the other hand, has the same particular tastes that I do.

What makes us family is that we all bring our personalities to the mix, and we appreciate, love, and respect the differences. We are also never short on innocent teasing and joking with each other about who does or does not do things just like Mom.

I am an affectionate person and give hugs and kisses in abundance to my children. When they were young, my children loved the hugs and kisses, but as they grew, they preferred varying degrees of affection. My oldest was very much like me, and she loved the hugs and kisses. She still does. My son was receptive as long as we weren't in public, and my youngest was not always in the mood for the affection I wanted to bestow. I had to adjust. With my son, when he saw me wanting to give him a kiss, he would lean the top of his head over so I could place a kiss there. That became a special sign of affection for us. With my youngest daughter, I would express my need to give her a hug or kiss, she would see that look on my face, and she would let me hug or kiss her until she'd had enough and then would say, "Okay, Mom."

As my children were growing up, especially the younger ones, they would occasionally get in their head that I expected them to be like an older sibling, especially if they were being disciplined. My child might say, "I am not Meghan" or "I am not Matt," referencing a sibling.

I would respond, "I don't want you to be anyone but yourself because I already have a Matt [or a Meghan or a Mary Kate]. I do not need another one of those. I need you to be the best that you can be." That would always be my response to them as I reminded them, "You are who you are, and I love you for who you are."

All I wanted was for my children to be themselves. Share a similar message with your children. They need only to be themselves, and you will love them for it.

What Are Their Interests and What Are Yours?

In loving your children unconditionally, you are accepting differences in your children. You have to be aware of their interests and find ways to share in those interests. If there is something that you are interested in that your children are not, find a way to introduce that interest to them. Maybe they will start to like it; maybe they won't. Either way, you will have spent time with them.

If there is a hobby or activity they really enjoy, take an interest in that as well. When you take an interest in something that they are interested in, it shows that you love them unconditionally. You love them and want to spend time with them and want to learn or share this thing that means something to them. By accepting your child for the person that he or she is, for the person that God created, for the person that God blessed you with, you exemplify unconditional love.

When it comes to sports, I am not a fan at all. When I was in school, physical education (or PE) day was the most dreaded day of the week. When my children started playing sports, I found ways to get involved even though I was not a sporty girl at all. Many times, I served as team mom just so I could share that activity with my child. You can find ways to volunteer for your child's activities too. If it is a sport you have played, you can volunteer to coach, you can be a team mom, or you can help at practice.

Be creative, and you will discover many ways you can take an interest in activities important to your child, even if the activities are not things you particularly enjoy doing on your own. Anytime you get involved in something your child is doing, you are telling your child, "Since this means something to you, it means something to me." That shows unconditional love.

When I was growing up in Colorado, I was a Camp Fire Girl. Back then, you were either a Camp Fire Girl or a Girl Scout. They were almost two opposing teams. Of course, Camp

Fire Girls had faded in popularity by the time I had Meghan. She wanted to be a Daisy in kindergarten and then become a Brownie, which were both a part of Girl Scouts. I did not know anything about Girl Scouts because I had not been a Girl Scout, having been a Camp Fire Girl instead.

I had to take an interest in and learn all about Girl Scouts. I even got to the point where I volunteered to be a cookie manager. If you know anything about Girl Scout cookies, you know that when that time of year comes and those boxes of cookies are everywhere, it is intense and a big undertaking. For days, our garage was filled with Girl Scout cookies while parents came to pick them up, and hours were spent scheduling cookies sales, collecting money, and accounting for it all. Despite the intense commitment, I volunteered as a way to get involved in something important to my daughter. Whatever it is, whatever your children's interests are, seek out and embrace those opportunities to get involved, share those interests with them, and in doing so, demonstrate your unconditional love.

Never Compare

Never compare your children. This I cannot say too strongly. *Never compare your children.* When you compare your children, you are immediately taking away acceptance of them. You are taking away that unconditional love. You are basically saying—and they get the message—that they should be more like Susie or Sammy, and Mom does not love them as much because they are not that child.

I will talk about this in more depth in an upcoming chapter, but at this point, just be aware that comparing your children and unconditional love do not go together. Children should be loved in their own right, not in comparison to anybody else. That test will come someday, as mentioned earlier, when your child says, "You only want me to be like [insert sibling's name]."

Your children will test you with those words, and you should be able to say, "I do not want you to be like your brother or sister. I love you for who you are. That will never change, but I am going to do everything I can so that you are the best you can be."

When I was growing up, I experienced what it was like to be compared. I know there was no malicious intent behind it. It was more a sign of the times and a lack of awareness of the effects of comparison on a child. Today, there is more information available about the psychology of parenting. I knew who the favorites were, and I wasn't one of them. This was hurtful because I felt that I didn't measure up. I felt that anything I did would not be enough because I was not the favored child in my parents' or grandparents' eyes. A remark as simple as "Look at how your sister did this; you should do it that way too" is a comparison. Even though you are not voicing the words "I am comparing you to your sister," it is happening. "Your brother did this. Isn't that wonderful? Why don't you do things more like that?" That is comparing your children.

You should never, never, never compare your children. If this is something that you are doing now, please take steps immediately to change that behavior because it kills self-esteem and negates any feeling of unconditional love. Your children will feel they are not loved as much as a sibling. Find those unique, lovable traits in each of your children and focus on those.

When something is happening for one child, it is okay to say something to that child in the presence of another child, as long as you don't make the other child feel like he or she is being compared. If you are going to say something about one child in front of another child, make sure that you say something nice and loving about the other child as well. All of your children should feel loved.

Just a couple of weeks ago, I was standing in a coffee shop. I had placed my order and was waiting for my drink to be prepared when I noticed a mother with two young children in line. Her son was older, around six years old, and her daughter was maybe two or three years old. The daughter wanted to hold her mom's hand so badly. Every time she would take her mom's hand, her mother would jerk it away and say, "No." The daughter would try again, and the mother would say, "No." From what I could tell, the daughter had misbehaved, and because of that, the mother was not going to allow her child to hold her hand.

If this mother was loving her child unconditionally, she would have held that child's hand. There are other times and other ways to deal with misbehavior. By keeping her hand from that child, she was conditionally loving her child, and then she continued by saying, "See, your brother knows how to behave; your brother gets to hold my hand."

That just broke my heart. That poor little girl just loved her mom and just wanted to know that her mom loved her unconditionally in return. At that moment, the mom was not showing unconditional love and was even going so far as to compare her children.

As a mom, you never want to speak ill of your child—ever. Just do not do it. If you are talking to your child or disciplining him or her, or there is something that the child needs to change about his or her behavior, that is different. In those cases, you are voicing your concerns to the child directly. What you don't want to do is converse with a friend or family member and speak ill of your child to them. Talking about behaviors is one thing; talking about a child in a negative way is a completely different thing. Your child should be unconditionally loved.

If you are speaking ill of your child, then that habit needs to be corrected or changed. It is okay to say, "I had an issue with Sammy talking back, and we corrected that behavior through time-out." Moms get advice from each other, and there is nothing wrong with that. What I mean about not speaking ill of your child is that you should avoid saying, "My child is not smart at all" or "my child cannot ever behave" or "my child is a whiny brat." Those are things that you do not ever want to put out into the atmosphere. Remember the message to your child: *you are who you are, and I would not want it any other way.*

Accept It All: Flaws, Strengths, Personality

Unconditional love means acceptance. Accept your child, his flaws, his strengths, and his personality. When I was growing up, I had a very close relationship with my grandparents. Just being around them meant feeling that acceptance and love. Whatever my flaws and strengths were, I knew that I had their love unconditionally and was accepted.

When there is a personality difference between child and parent, that can present a difficulty. Sarah is a mom who is very successful in her career, and because of that, she compartmentalizes her emotions. When her daughter was born, she was a little one who needed to cry to feel better when she was sad. Because Sarah saw that as a weakness, she often commanded her daughter not to cry. The little girl was told not to shed tears, and that stifled her emotions.

Acceptance is recognizing and appreciating personality characteristics in your children, not expecting or forcing them to conform to your personality. If you have a child who needs to show her emotions through tears, let her. Crying is a healthy expression of emotion, and there is nothing wrong with a child shedding tears, even if that is different from how you as a mom would express your emotions.

I am an outgoing person, and when my oldest daughter was young, she was very shy around others. That was an adjustment for me. I had to support Meghan's personality and, at the same time, push her a little bit to help her become comfortable in new situations and with new people. I had to accept that she was going to be shy and a bit more reticent in her conversation with others, but that was okay because that was who she was. Supporting her while pushing her gently out of her comfort zone was just the right mix. Today as an adult, she is very comfortable in social situations and is actually very outgoing.

I am a planner and organizer, and when my son was younger, he sometimes behaved like an absentminded professor. Matthew was very intelligent, but because he had his mind on so many important things, he sometimes was forgetful. I had to accept my son as he was, even though at times it could be frustrating when he would forget things—where his cleats were, where his homework was, or what time he had to be at practice. We worked through any challenges his forgetfulness might cause, and all the while, I was accepting of and loving toward my son.

When I was growing up, I never would have thought of saying to my parents in anger over limits and rules, "I hate you!" Once my youngest daughter reached preschool age, she began saying those words when she got angry at me, usually because I was putting limits in place. As her mom, I had to accept that Mary Kate was angry, but I also let her know that this was not an acceptable way to express her feelings when she was angry. In her moments of distress and anger, as she was telling me she hated me, I would calmly respond, "I still love you even though you say you hate me. I still love you, so let's think about what you are really upset about."

I helped Mary Kate express her emotions appropriately, but also I loved her. Do not be the mom who retaliates with "I hate you too." You cannot do that since you are the one showing your child the proper way to live and respond to things. Your job is to help your child express her feelings in a healthy way and still love her even though she is expressing herself in a way that you would prefer she didn't. Encourage your child to express her feelings differently, and she will learn to do that over time.

Acceptance does not mean accepting bad behavior; your child will not be allowed to behave poorly. Acceptance means that you will love your child in spite of that behavior and encourage and help your child to turn that behavior around and improve. You will not have a condition that when your child behaves better, you will love him. That kind of thought process will not foster unconditional love. The thought process must be that you love your child, and you will work with him to make things better and improve the behavior. The behavior is separate from the child.

Discipline and Love Connection

As an educator, I have spent many years in the classroom. When I was in the classroom with middle-school students, I would ask students why they thought their parents disciplined them. "Why do your parents discipline you? What is the purpose behind it?"

In every instance, the students recognized that through discipline, their parents were showing their love for them. They told me that if their parents did not care, they would not discipline them. By disciplining their children, these parents are showing that they have an interest in the people their children are going to become. They love their children and want them to be the best that they can be. Discipline is part of love, and children recognize that even at middle-school age, when they tend to test those limits. They will push back against their parents' rules, but they recognize that those rules are a way that their parents show their love for them.

It is not fun or easy to discipline your children. Still, it is a necessary part of being a parent and showing that unconditional love for your children. It is by disciplining them that you are helping them become the best that they can be.

When you are disciplining your child, the most important thing is to focus on the behavior and not the child. When you are able to separate those two, focusing on the behavior, you help your child understand that it is the behavior that needs to change. You are sending a message to your child: *It is this behavior that I dislike or this behavior that I am not going to allow to continue. It has nothing to do with you as my child, the child whom I love and treasure, but the behavior has got to go.*

The reason you want to make the distinction between the behavior and the child is that behavior is something your child can change. He cannot, however, change who he is at his core. We are the people that we are. Separating the behavior from the child makes the child recognize that you still love him even though you are angry or disappointed in his behavior.

Remember that your child is not bad, even when the behavior is. I always cringe when I am at the grocery store, for instance, and I hear a mom say to her child, "Stop being so bad." It is an easy thing to say, but the mom is probably not thinking about what she is saying and the message she is sending to her child. Your child is not bad. Your child is the child whom you love. When misbehaving, your child is not bad; the behavior is bad. Make that distinction and be careful about your wording when you are disciplining your children.

Remember that you are the adult. Even though your children's behavior can sometimes stress you beyond your limits or patience, you must remain the adult in your actions. If you have your own meltdown and let out your own frustrations in front of your children, then you are on their level. That is disconcerting for them and does not help them. It makes them feel unsure of the world when they see their mom, to whom they look for assurance that things will be okay, having a meltdown and losing control of her feelings.

It is okay to say to your child, "You know, I am really disappointed in what you just did. I am angry. I need to take a moment, and then we are going to talk about it." It is okay to get a handle on your emotions first because you should never discipline when your anger is in control. When anger is involved, you will not discipline the best way that you should. You should be responding to the behavior, not reacting to it. When you react in the moment, it is possible to say or do something you will later regret.

Respond to what the child has done; respond to the behavior and address that behavior. You are not angry at the child, remember; you are angry at the behavior. If your child is misbehaving or doing something that you do not want him or her to do, you can think about how you will word it and respond to your child in an appropriate way. To stress the point, the behavior can be bad, but the child is not. Often that is a difficult thing to remember in the heat of the moment.

Take the time you need to step back and get a handle on what actually happened. If Tommy took the scissors to the family pet, instead of saying that he is bad, you could say, for example, "Tommy, it is not acceptable to take the scissors and cut Spot's fur." In doing so, you address the behavior without calling the child bad. You let him know that what he did was an unacceptable behavior. You can go on to say, "That behavior is wrong, and you need to think about what you did. That is not acceptable, and I will not allow you to do that again."

Decide the disciplinary measure you want to use, and communicate that and the reason for it. Time-out is an excellent measure, and a good rule of thumb is one minute for each year of age. You would continue the conversation with three-year-old Tommy by explaining, "You are going to sit in time-out for three minutes because you cut Spot's fur, and you need time to think about that."

If you focus the attention on Tommy and say that he is a bad boy for cutting the dog's fur, then you will chip away at Tommy's self-esteem. You will send a clear message that you think he is bad instead of letting him know that the behavior is bad. There is a distinct difference between "It is unacceptable that you took the scissors and cut the dog's fur" and "You are a bad boy because you cut the dog's fur." Always focus on the behavior, not the child. Take every step to preserve your child's self-esteem because that is part of unconditional love.

Building a Strong Foundation

Of all of the gifts that we give our children, the premier gift is unconditional love. All of the other gifts are built on top of that foundation. Love your children so that your children know they are loved unconditionally.

When you focus on the child and on always making him or her feel unconditional love, you are making sure that everything else that your child does, everything else that you do, and everything else in your relationship is built on that foundation. I have seen the damage when that unconditional love is missing. When children do not feel loved unconditionally, they feel less valued and less worthy, and it chips away at their self-esteem. It impacts relationships in their family, with their friends, and throughout their lifetime.

Ensure that your children know and feel that they are loved unconditionally. Once that is in place, all the other gifts will build on top of the unconditional love. Recently, I was watching a reality show, one in which the participants were trying to improve their lives by getting healthy. The young man who was the subject of the episode had very low self-esteem and felt so poorly about himself. The young man poured out his feelings to the coach about never feeling love from his parents, about always feeling like he was not worthy of love and not valued enough.

Remember that you are your children's world. You are the one whom they expect to love them unconditionally. If that is not happening, your children will think, *Of all the people in the world, my mom should love me, and if my mom does not love me, then I am obviously not worthy of love.* In that reality show, that was the thought process of the young man— an outpouring of words about his lack of self-worth and never feeling like his mom loved him enough.

When I was teaching in the Midwest, I taught a student who was experiencing a lot of turmoil because of his parents' separation and divorce. The student was living with his father and stepmother. He had distance from his mom. When he was with his mom on rare occasions, he did not feel that she cared enough, and he wondered, *How could she let me go and not feel like she needs to be a part of my life?* This impacted him in the classroom, and I tried to help him work through it because I could see the lack of self-esteem. I tried to help him achieve the potential that I knew he had. At his core, he had programmed himself to believe he could not achieve because he was not worthy—because his mom did not love him. That is how powerful your love is in the lives of your children; that power must be a positive force achieved through unconditional love.

Abandonment is something that is very difficult for children to get over. You might not be able to be with your child all of the time, but you can still send the message of unconditional love to them: *You are important to me, I value you, I love you, and I want to be in your life and have you in my life as much as I can.*

Chapter Two
The Gift of Intrinsic Motivation

*Motivation is a fire from within. If someone
else tries to light that fire under you,
chances are it will burn very briefly.*
—Stephen R. Covey

Lack of Motivation and How It Manifests

You can probably think about adults in your life today who lack motivation. These adults are shunning responsibility at work, are not taking responsibility for their own mistakes, are trying to get others to do work that they should be doing, or are trying to take credit for things that they did not do. There are people who cannot keep a job and who always think that their boss does not like them and so quit their current job and try to find a better one. There are people who always think the grass is greener on the other side, who are always looking for the easy way out, or who are always looking to find a job that will not expect too much of them.

Those adults serve as reminders of what lack of motivation looks like and how it manifests itself. Do not raise your children to have this lack of motivation. Intrinsic motivation is a crucial gift to give your children so that they will not grow into adults with a lack of motivation.

I have seen in my own life people who have so much potential; they are bright and have so much going for them. Yet they can't hold a job, they play video games all day, or they do not take on work or responsibilities that they are totally capable of doing. Maybe they cannot take direction from a boss or superior, so they have a hard time functioning in the work world. You have seen it, a friend who keeps going through job after job because he did not like that the boss made a decision he didn't agree with or did not like that the boss required him to work. In the classroom, I have seen very capable children failing classes because they do not want to put forth the effort to do better. Ensure that your children do not become adults like this; raise them with the gift of intrinsic motivation, and they won't.

When I was growing up, societal norms about child-rearing were not the same as they are today, and my parents raised me very differently than what is the norm today. I was raised with the expectation that I would pull my weight, and I had responsibilities within the family. If I ever got in trouble in school and went home to tell my parents about that, they never expressed that it was my teacher's fault. Instead, their response was "You are going to fix this." The thought never occurred to them that the teacher might have done something wrong; it was something I did. That would be followed by specific expectations of what I would do to correct the behavior. "You will go into school tomorrow, and it will be a different day."

Today's societal norms are the exact opposite. Parents are too quick to make excuses for their children or rescue their children. What you have to remember as moms is that when you rescue your children or make excuses for them, you are not doing them any favors, and you are not teaching them that it is important to do the right thing and work within society. The school is their first society; that is their work world, and behaviors that they learn there will later translate to their jobs and careers.

Today, too often adults are too quick to reward their children. Moms are too quick to reward, teachers are too quick to reward, and society is too quick to reward. When you reward too quickly and then the reward is gone, what will motivate the child? If children are not getting an outside reward, then what will motivate them? Children must have that built-in intrinsic motivation. If they have that, it will not matter what rewards are or are not out there extrinsically; they will still fulfill their responsibilities, work hard, and find success. Your children will be driven to excel because they will feel that motivation from within.

As an educator, I have seen so many problems when intrinsic motivation is missing. For years, I have taught gifted and talented students. Most people in the world think that gifted and talented students will automatically excel and do well; they will have that intrinsic motivation to do well. However, this is not always the case.

The saddest thing is when you know the child is capable, such as a child who has been identified as gifted and talented. Such children have exceptional qualities and talents, and yet some of them come into the classroom failing courses because they are not turning in homework. They are choosing not to do the projects, or they are doing them halfway in a shoddy manner. They are choosing to take the easy way out. They do not want to put forth the effort. That is what happens when a child is not intrinsically motivated.

Often, I would have students, even gifted and talented students, whose parents wanted to intervene for them when they weren't meeting their responsibilities, and yet the students didn't even care. The parents would call me requesting special treatment or extra credit so their child could pull up his grade. Then when the child was given that opportunity, the student did not even care and would not complete the extra-credit assignment. Mom was reacting and wanted to help her child change his grade, but the child had no interest whatsoever. In cases like this, the children are not intrinsically motivated. It does not matter what their moms want; the children do not feel the need to comply because it is not important to them.

I see so many rewards—the stickers, the trophies, and so on. It is overkill. Maybe the parents think that their children must get a trophy for joining a club or playing on a team or that they must be rewarded with a sticker for completing their homework. Those rewards on occasion can be fine, but when you reward too often, you are sending your child the message that the child needs to do a good job only if there is going to be something in it for him or her. If your child learns to do his best only if he receives an outside reward, he will not have intrinsic motivation.

As a teacher in the classroom during standardized state testing, I saw capable students sitting in their seats and not reading the questions, but just going down the row and randomly bubbling answers. Such students would then put their heads down, saying they were done, while there was still plenty of testing time remaining. These students had the potential to score really well, and it was sad to see them choose in that moment not to do the work because they were not going to get anything for it. You could see the wheels spinning: *What is this standardized test going to do for me?* Intrinsic motivation was missing; they had no desire to do their best for the sake of it.

On the flip side of that are the students who will not accept anything less than perfection. Maybe they feel they have to be perfect, but that is not the message you want to send your children. Intrinsic motivation is not about being perfect. It is about doing your best and feeling pride in a job well done. Never would you want to make your children think they have to be perfect. Does it really matter if that A is 100 percent? Isn't a 93 percent an A as well? If they want that A, and that is what they are working toward, then celebrate the success of achieving that A and let them know how proud you are whether they earn a 93 or a 100.

Do not instill in your children a need to be perfect because no human is perfect. If you make your children feel like they have to be perfect, then they are always going to be setting themselves up for failure. That is not what intrinsic motivation is about. You want the expectations to be reasonable. You want them to be able to set expectations that are challenging but achievable and then have pride in that job well done.

What Is Intrinsic Motivation?

Intrinsic motivation is, at its core, when a child is motivated by her own sense of feeling pride in a job well done. It is her sense of putting in effort, doing a good job, and being proud of what she has done. It is that internal desire to do well, that internal desire to want to do her best. Part of intrinsic motivation is working through challenges and finding success, and there is nothing more empowering for a child than that.

It is hard to see your children struggle and feel frustration, but a lot of damage can be done if you are quick to rescue your children. If your child never struggles or never faces a challenge as a child, he never learns to develop those skills necessary to overcome and face challenges as he grows. Then when he becomes an adult and is faced with that first moment of not being successful, he is likely to throw his hands up in the air and not know how to proceed.

When your children show frustration over something they are trying to do at school or a new skill they are trying to learn, that is okay. Even if they shed a few tears because they are really challenged and frustrated, that is fine. Help them work through that frustration and challenge. Let them know that you believe in them and their ability to work through the challenge. Especially when they are younger, you can help them think of ways to push through that barrier or challenge and meet success.

When they do finally meet that success, there is nothing more empowering to a child than being able to say, "This was so hard, but I worked through it! I did it!" Such opportunities are very powerful for building intrinsic motivation. You want your children to focus on how important it is to do their best and work toward a job well done. That is so much more important than rushing it.

As children are instilled with intrinsic motivation, this desire to do well on their own, they will begin to focus on the thought of doing their best even if it takes a little longer. They will learn not to rush things just to say they finished. The children in my classroom who just wanted to be finished with the test would turn in their tests with half of the answers missing. The test might have several short-answer questions worth many points, and yet students would submit these assessments with no response at all. Those were the questions that required some time and effort, and the students just did not feel like putting in the time and effort to complete them. These students were failing to answer not because they didn't have the ability to answer; these students were not answering because that was their choice.

Intrinsic motivation helps the child to recognize that this sort of choice is not the choice he wants to make. Instead, he wants to feel the pride in completing the questions, working through the difficulty, and challenging himself to be thorough. He can feel good after putting down an answer, even if it is not the correct answer, because he knows he has tried his best.

Frustration and Challenge Are Okay

As mentioned earlier, frustrations and challenges are okay. Do not rescue your child in order to prevent her from feeling challenged or frustrated. Help your child cope with frustrations and challenges in a positive way by helping her recognize that challenges and frustrations are a natural part of life. We all meet challenges, even into adulthood.

When you encounter challenges yourself and successfully address those challenges and adjust to them, you are helping your children by showing them that we all experience these things. You are demonstrating positive and effective ways to work through challenges. You are instilling intrinsic motivation in your children when you allow them to rely on themselves and their own abilities to work through challenges. Your children will be empowered when they see the end result. They will be empowered when they recognize that they faced a difficulty, worked through it, and were successful.

A few years ago, I went to a conference for educators of gifted and talented students. That day, the student speaker was a young man of about thirteen. He shared his love of learning and his successes in a gifted and talented program and said, "Learning is not always fun." I was so impressed with what he said that I wrote it down. Here was a gifted student, obviously very intelligent, sharing his love of learning but at the same time recognizing that it isn't always fun.

Challenges are encountered by everyone, even students who are gifted and talented. Your children do not need rescue from this; they need experience getting through it. Yet society has changed. When I was going to school, the last thing I expected when I went to school was that it was going to be fun. Maybe some fun things would come out of that day, but mostly, I was going to school to learn. The tide has turned and not necessarily for the better when the message sent to your children is that they should have fun at school all day, and if the students are not having fun, then the teacher is doing something wrong.

The reality is that life is not always fun. Adults in the work world see this every day. Some days on the job are better than others. Some days you just have to go to work because that is how you get paid. That paycheck provides for your family and puts food on the table, but it will not necessarily be fun earning every single dollar of it.

Adults have to do a job because they are hired to do a job. When at work, you do the best job that you can. Make sure that your children receive that message from their youngest years onward. Learning is not always fun, but that does not mean that learning is not important.

In the classroom, I am a challenging teacher, and I have high expectations of my students. My favorite quote is by Charles Kettering: "High achievement always takes place in the framework of high expectations." My students know that I am going to expect a lot of them. I will not expect something from them that they cannot achieve, but I will expect them to work hard to achieve the best within them.

A few years ago, I had a student who was being challenged in my classroom, and he was feeling it. As he was adjusting to my expectations, his grades were dropping, and he was frustrated. He knew he needed to make changes to pull up his grades. He counseled with me to work to my expectations, he began putting forth great effort, and he worked through the challenge. On every assignment he completed, he worked to do his best, and he took great pride in showing me that he was willing to put forth that effort. At the end of the year, I had a note from his mom: "My son learned so much from you and feels so lucky to have had you as a teacher. It amazes me that getting a double exclamation point comment from you on his work is more important to him than a 100%. I wish I could learn how to do that as his mom."

I never wanted my students or my children to think it was about perfection. You do not want to make your children feel they have to be perfect. You do, however, want them to know that they will face challenges, that they will have to work to that challenging level, and that they will always be expected to do the best that they can do. My philosophy has always been this: even if you do not meet my high expectations, you are better off working to that level and doing the best you can because even if you fall short, you will have achieved more than if I expected less of you.

A very important part of intrinsic motivation is to feel the challenge, work through that challenge, and be empowered by that challenge. Tears are empowering. When your children are crying because they are frustrated over a challenge, support them, but don't rescue them. As they work through those tears, as they pull themselves together, they are proving to themselves, *I am not going to let that frustration win because I can do this.*

When I was in sixth grade, I had to create a visual aid for my project on Mary Bethune. We had just moved to Georgia, I had just started at a new school, and one of my first assignments was this project. I did not feel very creative, and it was stressful for me whenever I had to do anything creative. The assignment was to research our subject and create a visual aid that symbolized that person.

As I was working on this Mary Bethune project, I decided to create an elementary school building. I had a vision in my head of what this school should look like, but I just could not get it to look the way I had it pictured in my mind. I did not believe in my own creative ability to do it. I was sitting on the floor, growing increasingly frustrated, and the tears were flowing. My dad walked through the room, saw me crying, and said, "Trudi, why are you crying?"

I answered, "I cannot get this project to look the way that I want. I can't do it!"

My dad did not step in and try to help me. He did not come over to me and do anything. He just looked at me and said, "You will be able to work through it, and I know you will get it done."

I wiped away my tears, took a deep breath, and finished that project. It was done entirely with my creative hands. It was not beautiful, but I was able to complete the project, and that was empowering to me. I was frustrated by that project, and I really did want to throw my hands in the air in despair. But my dad let me know that I could do it, and I did.

When my daughter Meghan was in high school and struggling through geometry, every night the homework would cause tears. She was a straight A student, and the thought of a B on her report card was hard for her to accept. Through the tears, she would tell me that geometry was too hard. I worked with her and helped her recognize that even though geometry was difficult for her, she could take some steps to get through it successfully. I offered solutions such as talking to her teacher, asking for extra help, or hiring a tutor, but I never said to her that this was not worth working through. I never said that this was not worth finding the strength within, meeting the challenge, and doing her best. It was not about perfection.

For students who strive for As all of the time, it can be distressing to get a B. You have to help them see that it is not the end of the world. The message to your children should be that if they have done their best and have put forth every effort they can, and that is the grade they get, then there is no shame in that.

How to Focus Praise

When your child excels or accomplishes a goal that he has been working hard toward, focusing praise appropriately will help him learn intrinsic motivation. If your immediate response is to jump in and shower your child with material things such as gifts or money, then you have taken away in that instant the reward of pride in a job well done. If you recognize that you are one to jump in and buy your children presents or tell them they earned a gift or reward, take the steps to scale back on that so that the first response can be joy and pride in a job well done.

Focus your praise on the doing. If they have worked hard on something and have done well at it, focus on that process. When my kids would accomplish a goal or excel at an activity,

I would say to them something like "You studied really hard for that test and put in a lot of hours of work. Look at what you accomplished because you did that. You should be very proud of yourself for earning an A on that test!" Instead of saying that I was so proud of them, my first response would be "You should be so proud of yourself!"

Instill in your children the understanding that they worked for those achievements. They did that! They should feel pride, and when they feel pride, that is part of intrinsic motivation. If your child is trying out for a team, putting in lots of extra hours at practice, and working hard at honing those skills that she knows she needs to make the team, and then she makes the team, your child should hear you say, "You should be so proud of yourself; you worked so hard! Look at all the hours you put into practicing that skill. Look at what you accomplished because you did that; you made the team!"

Focus on the doing and not on the specific outcome in that moment. The process that your child worked through to achieve her goals is where the praise should be directed. Even if she does not make the team, it is still empowering if you focus on the process that she put into it. This helps the child recognize that it was a process, not just something that she could walk in and get or something just given to her. Children must work for an accomplishment, earn it, work through the frustrations, and put in the effort to achieve.

Children will be intrinsically motivated when they learn that they are the ones in control of whether they achieve something or not. It is not about you doing it for them or you rescuing them or you giving them unneeded support. It is you allowing them to work through that process and encouraging them along the way but letting them do it. Remember that go-to phrase: "You should be so proud of yourself because _____." Continue the praise by focusing on what they did and helping them recognize what they achieved.

When Meghan graduated from eighth grade, she was showered with award after award at the graduation awards ceremony. We were taken aback. Every single award was earned because of something Meghan had worked hard to achieve. In congratulating her, I said, "You should be so proud! You earned these awards and scholarship because of your hard work and effort." I did not say to her, "What an awesome kid you are. Look at everything you won!"

It was important to turn the focus back on the hard work that she had done to achieve her awards. "You put in the time and effort and accomplished these things, and you should be proud of that!"

Is There a Place for Extrinsic Motivation?

The balance has to be that primarily you are helping your children learn intrinsic motivation. You want them to do things because they feel that sense of pride, they do not want to do anything less than their best, and they are always looking for a job well done. Then if they are intrinsically motivated and you want to reward them extrinsically, that is just icing on the cake. They do not need that extrinsic motivation; they were not counting on that in order to do their best. It is something that your children were not expecting and that now they are getting. Maybe you offer an ice cream as an extra reward or a movie outing. Extrinsic rewards on occasion are fine if the main point is that your children are intrinsically motivated. You don't want your children to do something only to get some outside, extrinsic reward.

When we were raising our children, we clearly communicated the expectations for grades in school. If we had known that their doing their best meant they would get Cs, that would have been fine with us, but we knew that our children were capable of more than that. They knew that we did not expect *all* As, but we did let them know that we expected As and Bs. We wanted them to strive for As because, in most cases, we knew they were capable of that.

We did not pay for grades; we did not want them to be motivated by the extrinsic reward. We wanted them to work for those As because they wanted to do their best, because they were capable of achieving those grades, and because they would feel proud of working hard and seeing their report card with As on it. We did not want them to achieve just because they would get paid for those grades.

On the other hand, my dear friend Tessa had a different motivational tool for her daughter. Whenever report cards were issued, her child received five dollars for every A. Tessa would say to me, "It is no different than when my child will have a job and earn bonuses for a job well done." True. In many careers, bonuses are sometimes awarded for a job well done. However, do employees always get bonuses for a job well done? Not usually. More often than not, a bonus is something that can be earned, but that might not always be an easy thing to do. In addition, these are often annual or semiannual rewards. What about the day-to-day motivation? For my husband and me, it was more important that our children learn that their grades were a reflection of how hard they worked, how much they strived to reach excellence, and how much effort they put into overcoming challenges and doing their very best.

When our children came home with grades, we did have a ritual to highlight their achievements. When they came home with their report cards, I would sit down privately with each one. This was not a matter of announcing, "Oh, Johnny got all As, and Susie got all Bs."

We did not publicize each child's grades to the whole family. I would take each child, one by one, and we would sit down with his or her report card. It was such a special time with each child as we would talk about each grade. If it was a grade where we felt like she or he could do better, then I might say, "What do you think you could do differently next quarter to pull that grade up?" or "Do you think you did everything you could and did your best on everything, and this was the outcome?"

Sometimes I would hear, "No, Mom, I know I should have studied more, and my grade would have been better."

The purpose of the conversation was to let them know that each grade was a result of their effort and, especially when they did well, that they had worked hard to achieve those grades. "Think of all the things that you did—how hard you studied for tests, how hard you worked on projects, all those things you did to accomplish this grade. You were not just given this grade; you earned this grade."

If my children then chose to share with their siblings how they had done, that was up to them. When my husband came home from work that evening, the children would take pride in sharing their report cards with Dad as well. As a family, we would then go out to dinner. The celebration was not focused on whether one child got all As or they all got all As, but it was a reward for a whole quarter's worth of work on all of their parts. "It is the end of a grading period and time to celebrate all of the hard work. If you achieved what you strived to do, you should be proud of that. If you did not do as well as you wanted, it is a fresh start beginning tomorrow."

We all looked forward to those celebrations; however, these dinners were not a reward for grades. They were more a reward for the work done in finishing an important nine-week process, after which it was time to celebrate. That is how we rewarded our kids extrinsically while still keeping the focus on the intrinsic motivation we wanted instilled within them. Our children still got the message that the pride they felt in a job well done was the true reward.

Tasks That Elicit Bribery

Many tasks that you deal with as a mom, especially when raising young children, can easily lead to bribery to get your children to behave appropriately. Some of those tasks include shopping, long days spent running errands, waiting in doctor's offices, and eating out at restaurants. The bribery might occur because you are taking your children to a public place and you want to make sure that they will behave well and not throw a tantrum. Maybe you are meeting others, and you want your children to present themselves well, so you bribe them with an ice cream to encourage them to be quiet. Maybe you have to be in the car for a long time with your children, so you feel the need to bribe them to stay seated, buckled, and calm. At church, children must be quiet and not cry or scream, so you might bribe them to behave properly by offering candy or other treats.

The problem is that bribery does not help children learn intrinsic motivation. When you use bribery, as in giving your children something, an extrinsic reward for their behavior, you are teaching them that they should behave properly only when they will get something out of it. It is difficult to move away from that if it becomes the norm. If you are using bribery with your children, take steps to move away from rewarding for proper behavior. You will be happy you did, even though it will be difficult at first.

When I was raising my children and going through these exact same scenarios, I would sometimes think, *I cannot make it through this shopping trip if my children go into this store and start running amok.* So I understand completely, and I know why moms want to prevent that. Sometimes the only thing that moms know to do is to offer their children something to get them to behave so the mom can get through the shopping trip, car trip, or doctor's visit. It is not uncommon in any grocery store on any given day to hear a mom say, "You are not going to get candy if you keep that up" or "We are not going to get ice cream if you don't behave."

Although it might seem like bribery is the only option, it is not the best way to get your children to behave properly.

What you want to do instead is raise your children to behave properly because that is an expectation. It is not a negotiable point. The expectation is that they will behave properly, and you will address it if they do not. The expectation is the *proper* behavior. It should not be that the expectation is improper behavior, and therefore you need to bribe your children to prevent the improper behavior.

Do Not Routinely Reward Proper Behavior; Use Preparation

If you are not going to bribe your children, then how will you get them to behave properly? The best thing you can do to make sure your children behave properly is prepare them. It sounds like a simple thing that can't possibly work, but it will work. Once you get into the mind-set of using it, it will become second nature.

If I was going to the grocery store with my kids when they were little, I would say to them, "We are going to the grocery store; we are going to get only what is on my list. You will help me get things we need, or you will stay right with me so we can get through the grocery store as quickly as possible. It will not take long if you can stick with me and if we can stick to the list."

Then after you have prepared them, engage them. On those shopping trips with my children, I would let them help me find particular items on the shelf and put them in the cart. That way, I was creating an activity to engage them in the shopping process instead of having them sit in the cart and get bored. When boredom sets in, the chance for misbehavior increases.

If you are heading to church, you can prepare them by saying, "We are going into church. You need to be quiet and listen to what the priest has to say. You can read your books quietly, but you must stay in the pew and whisper if you need to tell me something. When it is time for communion, you will hold my hand and walk quietly with me."

Whether there is standing, sitting, or some other activity in your church, prepare them for that. Let them know what the expectation is. Then when you leave church, prepare them for what comes next. If they know what the expectation is, they can get in the mind-set of knowing what Mom wants and behave accordingly.

When I was a first-grade teacher and taught in a religious school, the students went to church services as a class once a week. Our class had one teacher, one aide, and thirty-three students. Those thirty-three first graders would sit in church with only two adults. I would space them so they were not right next to each other, and they would sit there, behave, and follow what they were supposed to do. We would guide them, giving little looks or hand gestures if they were doing something wrong or putting a hand on the shoulder if they needed some calming down. We did that on a regular basis. Even as a teacher, I used that preparation technique. I would say, "Okay, we are going to Mass. We are going to sit six to a pew, we are going to space ourselves out, we are going to keep our hands to ourselves, and we are going to listen. When Mass is over, we will return to the classroom, and it will be time for snack."

Preparation will work if you use it consistently. Your children will know the expectation, the reasonable length of time the activity will take, and what will happen afterward. They will know what that expectation is because you will be preparing them before they go in.

When our children were little, we traveled frequently. Most times it was going to see loved ones since we did not have a lot of extra money to take vacations. Most of our family members lived very far away; we moved around a lot because of my husband's job and never had the luxury of living near family members as we wished we could. We couldn't afford plane tickets often, so our travels usually consisted of long car rides as a family.

With three young children and car rides of ten, twelve, or fourteen hours, we had to prepare our kids for what the expectation was. I would talk about traveling far with many hours in the car and how each child could pack a bag with things to occupy her or himself. I would tell them when and where we would be stopping for the night. I explained that if they needed to go to the bathroom, they would need to give us plenty of notice so we had time to find a place to stop. We talked about stops for meals and things to look forward to when we arrived at our destination. We talked about stopping at the hotel and how they would get a chance to swim in the hotel swimming pool.

All of those details were meant to prepare them for the long car ride and let them know the expectations so that we could have an enjoyable trip. I had those conversations with them from a very young age. We never dreaded those trips even though we took several trips a year. We actually looked forward to the trips, all five of us in a car for an extended period of time. What better family bonding time could there be? We had wonderful conversations during those long-distance car trips, with our entire family in very close quarters.

To me, it was second nature that kids could go on long car rides with parents. Several years ago, my friend Becky asked me how to travel with her two small children for a long car trip home to visit family. "I can't even get my kids into the car for an hour without there being problems. They fight, cry, and make the trip very tiring. How will I survive a ten-hour car ride?" What I shared with Becky was that she could survive it and even learn to enjoy it. All she needed to do was prepare her children.

Again, preparation lets your kids know the expectations, but you must be prepared to follow through with discipline if you need to. Oftentimes, very little discipline is needed if your kids are properly prepared. You might have to remind them, "Remember—we talked about this. We are going to travel for a few hours, and you can read your books or play games, and then we will stop for lunch."

Recently, a family member was asking me how to prepare her kids for a long trip because they had done it only once before, and her children were not used to it. She explained how this long car trip was causing stress because her kids could not even make it a couple of hours together in the car. Her kids were older than mine had been when we started taking our children on long car trips. It all goes back to preparing them, getting them used to these things at an early age, and that becoming the norm of how they will behave.

Shortly after my second child was born, my paternal grandmother died. My son was only three weeks old, and my husband's work schedule would not allow him to take the time off. We lived at that time about seven hours from where the funeral was going to be held. I needed to attend; it was important to me. Yet if I went, I would be traveling alone with my three-year-old daughter and my three-week-old son. I was nervous about doing it by myself, but I knew I needed to do it.

Luckily, my husband's car had a bench front seat, and we did not have airbags then, so the children could ride in the front seat. There we were, young mom at the wheel, three-week-old son strapped in his car seat in the middle, and three-year-old daughter in her car seat next to him—all across the front seat— and off we went on a seven-hour car ride. During our stops for bathroom breaks, I also had to feed a three-week-old. I had prepared Meghan ahead of time by saying, "We will stop if Matthew needs to be fed, we will stop for lunch, and if you need to go to the restroom, we will stop for that. When we get there, we will stay with Papa and Great Gran, and we will get to see Grammy, Granddad, and your aunt and uncle."

I was nervous about it, but even at three years old, Meghan had made many long car rides before. It was not going to be the first time that I was putting her into the car for a long ride. We made it to the funeral, my children were happy and safe, and we had some bonding time in the car, again.

At one point, we were living in the Atlanta area, and my parents were living in the Chicago area. To get from one city to the other required a long fourteen-hour trip. Since I was a stay-at-home mom at that time, I had flexibility to travel when I wanted. Summer, when my kids were out of school, was the perfect time to make that trip. Unfortunately, my husband did not have the same flexibility, and his vacation time was limited. If I wanted to visit family, I often had to do that on my own with the kids. Many summers, I made that trip from Atlanta to Chicago, traveling in the car with my three children. For the trips to be successful, I had to prepare them.

"The halfway point is Bowling Green, Kentucky, so we will travel eight hours today. You will take things to keep you occupied. When it is lunchtime, we will stop and take a break. We will spend night one at the hotel and swim in the pool, and tomorrow, we will drive the rest of the way. Tomorrow night we will be at Grammy and Granddad's. We will have a few days of visiting, and we will find fun things to do in the city each day. It is important that you stay buckled up for the trip, and no fighting is allowed."

Preparing them always helped us have an enjoyable trip. When we visited someone else's place, I would also prepare them for the different rules of the household we were visiting. "You might see things out that look really pretty; you are not allowed to touch those things." I prepared them for what the environment would be like, what they would see, what they were allowed to do, and what the expectations were going to be. By doing that, I could ensure proper behavior.

When my children were a bit older, my husband was transferred, which required a move from Georgia to Connecticut. That required a very long trip in the car. He had to be there quickly for his new job, and we decided to let the kids finish at their old school and enjoy some summertime with their friends before we joined him. We wanted our children to start their new school at the beginning of the next school year so that they could make friends quickly and would not have to sit around all summer with no friends to play with.

When it was time for us to join my husband, we had a three-day cross-country trip, just me and my three children. We look back at that trip now as such a wonderful time for us since I had prepared the children. I had reviewed with them what the three-day trip would look like and how we had to do it. We were lucky that on one of the stops we were able to spend the night with family, which the kids had especially looked forward to.

As my children were growing up, much time was spent on long car rides, and that is not something that all parents enjoy doing. Long car rides can be tedious. For us, these trips were enjoyable and allowed precious moments with our children. Our children behaved properly because of preparation.

Preparation is also helpful when you are taking your children to church. The expectation in church is that children will be quiet, will listen, and will participate when needed. Children should not disturb other people who are there for worship. I know the easiest thing for a lot of people is to head to the cry room. I would encourage you not to do that. The reason is that if you raise your children to go to church in the cry room, then they never learn the proper behavior for church. Instead, use the cry room as a go-to place to address a behavior.

Prepare your child by telling him, "We are going to church today. Church will be an hour long, and you need to be quiet. You can take quiet activities with you such as books or coloring books." When children are young, this is fine since they do not really understand what is being said by the pastor. They can look at their books, do those quiet activities, and not bother the people around them. Prepare them to be quiet because people are there to worship God, and they need to respect that.

Let them know that this is the behavior you expect. If there is an outburst and you cannot quiet them immediately, then pick them up and take them to the cry room, where you can address the behavior. When they are calmed back down, take them back into church. Even though that is more work for you—having to get up, leave, and then return—in the long run you are better off, and so is your child. You will be teaching your children that what you want them to do is behave in church. They will be motivated to behave in church because you have prepared them for that.

Where does the reward come in? There is not a reward in the sense that you are going to give them something extrinsic. You will praise them because that goes a long way. When you have prepared them, and they have behaved well and done what you expected, tell them what a wonderful job they did. "We talked about how to behave in church, and you behaved exactly as you were asked to do. That was wonderful; you should be so proud of yourself!"

Remember they need to take pride in what they did. They accomplished something. You prepared them for how you wanted them to behave, they behaved that way, and now you are praising them for that proper behavior. In so doing, you help them feel proud of that.

Those first graders whom I would take to the pews? When we got back to the classroom, I would say, "You should be so proud of yourselves! You sat there so quietly, and you listened and participated at the right times. You were all so well behaved!"

I could see those little smiles on their faces as they realized they had done something so good. They were learning that intrinsic motivation: *I behaved properly. I did the right thing, and I should be proud of that.*

Intrinsic motivation and preparing your children are harder than simply using bribery, but in the long run, you will be better off. Avoid bribing your children to get them to behave properly. Instead, prepare and praise them.

The Importance of Intrinsic Motivation and How It Leads to Success

The whole point of intrinsic motivation is that your children learn to look within in order to succeed. As they go through life and become adults, you want them to look within themselves for motivation and not need or expect a reward if they do something right. Instead, you want the desire within to be their main motivator. The adults who cannot get their act together, who want others to do things for them, who can't hold a job, and who are not motivated to do their best are adults who are not intrinsically motivated.

Intrinsically motivated adults are crucial in a society that needs people who are willing to volunteer; people are not readily going to volunteer if they are not intrinsically motivated. With volunteerism, the motivation comes from feeling good about yourself and knowing you are doing something good for people, and that is felt within. Volunteers are not paid, so if you raise children who are not intrinsically motivated, where will the adults be to step up, lend a hand, and help out those who are less fortunate? When organizations need volunteers, people who are extrinsically motivated will be the last ones to volunteer because there is nothing "calling" them to do so. Nothing within is compelling them to help others simply for the sake of helping.

My children were raised to be intrinsically motivated; we were sparse on extrinsic rewards. On those rare occasions when they were rewarded extrinsically, the reward was simply icing on the cake and not the primary motivator. I raised my children to be proud of a job well done, to work their hardest, and to work through challenges. As adults now, all of my children have gone for advanced degrees, not because they had to do that or were getting paid to do that. They chose to do that because they wanted to further their education, achieve something greater, and give themselves every opportunity for more advanced work in their fields.

My daughter Meghan worked three jobs to put herself through graduate school and post-graduate school. She faced many challenges and had to do a lot of juggling of responsibilities to successfully work and earn her degrees. She was intrinsically motivated to earn those degrees, and so she worked through those challenges to do that.

My son set his sights on medical school and did everything necessary to get accepted. For years in medical school, his days consisted of a 24-7 study schedule with little free time and no rewards. He was intrinsically motivated to study hard because he wanted to do well on each and every test and in each and every class. That was enough to keep him putting in those hours and plowing ahead.

My daughter Mary Kate took a low-paying internship while in graduate school, which obviously was not for the monetary reward. She wanted to do her best, knowing that her internship could help advance her career if she worked hard and that she would learn valuable career skills in the process. The hard work and low pay were worth it in her mind because she was intrinsically motivated.

Rewards do not often come instantly in life, and the only thing that will keep your children working for that distant success is intrinsic motivation. Feeling pride in a job well done, feeling pride when they have put forth their best effort, and working toward the realization of their goals because of that pride are all part of intrinsic motivation. Raise your children to feel something within pushing them to do their best, pushing them to work through challenges, pushing them to behave properly. Intrinsic motivation will give them that inner calling to do their best and will be a gift of a lifetime.

Chapter Three
The Gift of Sibling Bonds

Siblings will take different paths and life may
separate them ... but they will forever be bonded
by having begun their journey in the same boat.
—Unknown

Bonds Do Not Happen Accidentally

The creation of sibling bonds is the third gift moms give their children, and this does not happen by accident. When I was raising my children, I wanted them to be close with their siblings. I recognized that there were things I could do to help make that happen, and my children today are best friends.

What does it look like when your children are best friends? They are supportive of each other, they encourage each other, and they genuinely care about each other. They want to see each other do their best and achieve great things. They do not look to bring each other down; they do not make another feel bad so that they can feel better.

Through the years, other people observing my children would ask how I got them to be so close. It was something that was at the core of my approach as their mom. I wanted them to see how lucky they were to have each other, and it paid off in their solid relationships today as adults.

What If My Child Has No Siblings?

If your child does not have a sibling, your child is still going to have a wonderful life. Your child might not have a sibling, but she or he will still have other important family relationships that can be nurtured. By nurturing those bonds, you will be creating supportive relationships for your child that will benefit your child throughout her or his life.

Both of my parents were only children. Even though my mom died when I was very young, I heard stories from her first cousin, who was exactly one year younger. Their birthdays were separated by three weeks. She told me how much she looked up to my mom, how she was her best friend, and how she always felt like my mom was the older sister she'd never had. They played like sisters, shared like sisters, and fought like sisters. Through it all, there was immense love. They were lucky because their parents lived near each other, which allowed them to see each other on a frequent and regular basis.

My mom's cousin loves to reminisce about how lucky she was to get my mom's hand-me-downs and how she looked forward to their sleepovers and their summers tanning together in the backyard. They vacationed together as families; they were very bonded and very, very close. Even though my mom did not have any siblings, she had a very tight bond with her cousin, and that bond felt as close to my mom as a sibling one.

My mom also had a male cousin who lived right up the street, another first cousin who was like an older brother to her. They were extremely close. My great-aunt had relayed stories of watching my mom come down the street carrying brownies to bring to her cousin. She loved spending time with him because they were so closely bonded. He was like the typical older brother and was protective of her since they attended the same high school and he knew who wanted to date her. In his eyes, no one was good enough for her. When that cousin was tragically killed in a car accident as a teenager, my mom felt as if she had lost her brother, and she grieved that loss for years.

Cousins, aunts, uncles, and close friends who feel like family can all provide those important relationships for your children. Even if your child does not have siblings, you can find other beneficial relationships that can give her that bond and nurturing. Children can never have too many people in their lives supporting them and creating close family ties.

My husband's parents had two other couples with whom they bonded as young adults because they lived in the same building on Long Island and were all young and newly married. As they all started having children, they raised their children side by side, and they seemed in many ways to be one giant family unit. The kids called those other adults aunt and uncle even though they weren't blood-related. They felt like they were family, and the children grew up feeling that way, and even after my husband's family moved to Louisiana, they stayed close.

Why Sibling Bonds Are Important

Your children's siblings are their first friends. They will be the friends who help each other weather life's challenges. They will be there for each other, often experiencing the same things at the same time. Because they are family, they will provide that supportive relationship when they are meeting life's twists and turns together.

When I was growing up, we moved quite frequently. Even though that could be unsettling, I knew that every time we moved, my sister would be there with me. Even though it would be difficult, and we would be sad leaving our friends, I knew that I had my sister, my built-in friend. While we were waiting to make friends at our new schools or in our new neighborhoods, I had somebody with whom I could play, share stories, talk, and share leisure time; I had a companion on life's journey. Some of my happiest childhood moments were moments I shared with my sister.

When my own children came along, I saw the same tight bond develop with them. When Meghan was in preschool, if I had an appointment or other commitment, I would sometimes drop Matthew off at the mom's-morning-out program at the same church. One day, Meghan's class was taken out to play in a large fenced area on the church property. She saw her brother with his group in another fenced-in area, and when Matthew saw Meghan, he started crying. He wanted to be with his sister so badly. He was missing home, and his sister was his connection.

When Meghan saw her brother crying, she started crying as well. She ran to the fence, he ran to the fence, and there they were—Meghan reaching through the links to touch her brother, Matthew reaching through the links to touch his sister, and both of them crying for each other. When I picked my children up that day, the preschool teacher said it was so heartwarming to see two siblings so bonded together. Meghan wanted to help her brother; she wanted to be with him because he was younger and sad. Matthew wanted to be with his sister because she provided a feeling of love and connection to home.

When my sister and I were moving around as kids, we always missed leaving friends, and we stressed each time we had to experience another first day of school. When we started at Warren T. Jackson Elementary School in Atlanta, I was in fifth grade, and my sister was in second grade. Our first day was in the middle of January, and we had been preparing for days. We wanted to make a good impression because starting school in the middle of the year is tough. We had just moved from Fort Worth, Texas, where maxi dresses were in fashion. We had new matching dresses, purple floral pattern, and we thought we would look so cute on our first day.

The first day of school, we showed up in our maxi dresses, and all eyes were on us as the other students wondered what in the world we were wearing. We looked at each other, and in that moment, we knew we had made a major fashion faux pas. Even though we were mortified in the moment, we laughed about it that night. We had experienced those looks together and had realized that the fashion trends in Georgia were not the same as in Texas, and we knew that even if it took a little longer to make friends, we at least had each other.

We had moved to a big house on a wooded lot with houses spread out down the street. We didn't have any neighborhood friends because it is hard finding friends when the street is too busy to play on. To top it all off, we were in a suburb of Atlanta, and we had to ride to school on a city bus, not a school bus, because the city was in the process of integrating schools and had contracted city buses to carry students to and from school.

My sister and I were terrified. It was the first time we had ever had to pay a dime and get on a city bus to go to school. We created a ritual to start each school day. We would get up each morning, make hot chocolate, pour it into cups, walk to the bus stop, and stand there drinking our hot chocolate while waiting for the bus to pick us up. Getting on that big city bus together made it easier for us because we were experiencing that fear and that challenge together.

When my mom died tragically shortly after the birth of my sister, there was a period of time during which my father had difficulty caring for three children right away. It was hard enough dealing with my brother and me at that time—two children under the age of five and a half. My grandparents stepped in and offered to care for my little sister to give my dad time to adjust. My dad also was working long hours, and a baby in the mix would have been too much. Even though my little sister was brand-new in my life, I knew that I missed her. Every day, I would stop at the door before going outside to play with my friends and say a prayer for my little sister. I prayed that she would soon be rejoined with our family so that I could see her every day.

Sibling bonds are a vital part of your children's lives, and you can begin nurturing these bonds at the earliest stages of development. Children learn their first social behaviors through interacting with siblings. When your children are learning to share with their siblings, they are learning skills that will help them make friends when they start school.

After Mary Kate was born, we quickly outgrew our house, which wasn't quite big enough for three small children. We recognized we needed to move, but houses didn't sell overnight. We thought we could get by for a few months, but as the house took longer to sell, we had to move to plan B.

Mary Kate had been making do in a small section of a room—a big closet almost. Although that had worked for her as a baby, it wasn't working as she grew into a toddler, and we needed an actual room for her. We asked Matthew if he would be okay with sharing his room with his little sister for a short while until we could move into our bigger house. He embraced the idea and was very thoughtful, readily accepting his sister into his room. He was excited to move into the top bunk so that she could have the bottom one. Through the experience, he learned that sharing space is something that we do in families.

Sharing with siblings prepares your children to share with others as well—friends, classmates, team members, and so on. Through sibling relationships, your children also learn the important value of taking turns. When children have siblings, they must learn to take their turn, whether they are playing a game, waiting in line, waiting to be tucked in, or waiting for Mom's attention. This crucial life skill is first learned from siblings.

Siblings also tend to be protective of one another. An older sibling may commonly protect a younger one, but also siblings as a whole, if they are raised in an environment that nurtures sibling bonds, are protective of each other. They look out for each other.

One Labor Day weekend, we decided to spend the long weekend in Maine as a family. We were sightseeing and happened upon a pier where we got caught up watching people haul in lobsters from the water. Mary Kate was intrigued and wanted to get a closer look. She walked near the end of the pier, with Matthew watching intently all the while. He grabbed her protectively because he was afraid she was getting too close to the end of the pier. Mary Kate was not going to fall in since we were watching her, and there was no way for her to get close enough to the edge to be in jeopardy, but in Matthew's mind, she was too close. He was in big-brother mode and was not going to let his little sister fall in the water.

One summer day, my children and I were at the neighborhood pool as part of our daily summer ritual. Meghan had jumped into the pool, and Matthew decided to do the same before I'd had time to put his water wings on him. When Meghan saw her brother trying to get his footing in the water, she grabbed him and pulled him up. Matthew had not even had a chance to realize he was in danger before his sister had come to the rescue.

Growing up, my children were always looking out for each other. When they were teenagers, the looking out for each other continued. When Mary Kate started dating someone in high school, my son was not impressed with the young man at all. Matthew felt she could do better, and he was not about to let it be. One day he picked her up from work with the intention of talking to her about the situation. She thought he was going to take her home; instead, he took a detour, told her he wanted to talk to her, and shared his feelings. He told her that he did not feel this guy was best for her and that she should be making different choices. He shared his concerns and the things he thought she should be doing differently. Even though she was not appreciative of his comments at the time, she recognized that he loved her and did not want somebody who was not worthy of her coming into her life. Still to this day, she talks about the time her brother took her riding in the car for the boyfriend lecture.

When Matthew was born, Meghan had a treasured blanket that she called Blankley; she took it everywhere. She was so thrilled with her new baby brother. She would put her pillow on the floor, lie on it with her baby brother, and cover him in her most precious possession, her Blankley. She treasured him even from those earliest moments. Sibling bonds are very powerful, and those bonds are a precious part of the family relationship.

What Moms Can Do

You might be thinking, *I recognize that sibling bonds are important, but how do I make sure that my children have them?* Before a sibling even arrives, you can take steps to create positive sibling bonds.

As you are shopping in preparation for the baby, talk to the older siblings about this new arrival and how precious this child will be in the family. Tell them how much this new baby will need his or her big brother and big sister. Share with them things they can do to help with the baby. That way, they feel like a part of the process. They will feel that this is a wonderful thing for them individually, not just for the family as a whole.

On the day I went to the doctor's office for a pregnancy test for my second pregnancy, Meghan was with me. She heard the confirmation that I was going to have another baby at the same time I did. From day one, she was part of that exciting news and had a positive view of the important addition to our family. She did not start out thinking, *Uh-oh! My mom is having another baby!*

During that pregnancy with Matthew, Meghan and I walked into a maternity store one day so I could get some much-needed maternity clothes. The woman who owned the shop approached me and asked, "Would you be interested in being in a fashion show in two weeks? We need moms to model our maternity clothes, and you would be perfect."

As I was standing there trying to process the unexpected request, the sales lady added, "We would really love for your daughter to do it too because we have some cute big-sister clothes that need modeling."

I accepted because I thought this would provide an exciting opportunity for Meghan to get into the role of big sister. She watched me model maternity clothes and was excited to help me as I changed from one outfit to another. She modeled a T-shirt with "Big Sister to Be" emblazoned across it. She was so proud of getting to hold my hand and participate in the fashion show as a big-sister-in-waiting to a little brother or sister who was about to be born.

When the new baby arrives in your family, prepare the older children. Be honest about changes, but help your children recognize that there will also be many things to look forward to with the new arrival. What you want to avoid is any jealousy of the new baby or your older children feeling displaced by this new sibling's arrival.

When Matthew arrived, Meghan was with friends; we had dropped her off there when I went into labor. After the delivery, my husband picked up Meghan and brought her to the hospital, stopping at the gift shop and allowing her to pick out a gift for her little brother. When they entered the hospital room, there I was, cradling my new son only hours old, and I invited Meghan to climb into the hospital bed with us. I watched her and listened to her as she expressed awe over his little fingers and little toes. She was lovingly stroking his head and giggling at his tiny features and movements, and in that moment, she saw him as nothing short of a blessing.

That moment was priceless. She learned from that first moment that she was not going to be set aside because her brother had joined the family. She was experiencing the joys of one big happy family, with her special place in the family still intact.

When Mary Kate was born, Meghan and Matthew were at my friend's house. We had dropped them off as we headed to the hospital. As soon as I could after the delivery, I made a personal call to my daughter and son, telling them on the phone, "You have a little sister!"

I wanted them to hear that exciting news from me, not a friend or anyone else. They had been waiting in anticipation, especially Meghan, since she was older. She had a brother already and was hoping so much for a little sister. When they later came to the hospital with my husband to meet Mary Kate, they were thrilled to see this new little member of our family.

In those early weeks, Mary Kate had colic, and anyone who has ever experienced that with a newborn knows how taxing it can be. I remember Meghan saying to me, "Mom, can Mary Kate stop crying? It is so loud!"

"Well, honey, she cannot really help it. She will grow out of it, but it will be a few weeks, and we just have to help her as much as we can until then. Remember how much you wanted a little sister?"

"Yes, but I did not want that one!"

To this day, we all laugh telling that family story. Meghan had wanted a little sister so badly, and then she had to adjust to the reality of this new little sister. Still, in the early days, that bond was starting. Even when she was thinking that this might not be exactly what she'd wanted, she loved her little sister, colic and all.

As your new children arrive, make sure that you have time alone with each of your older children. Believe it or not, time alone with each child corresponds with sibling bonds. You want to prevent any jealousy among siblings because jealousy among siblings will kill any sibling bond. Avoid that at all costs. If you spend time alone with each of your children, your children will see that each is loved and valued. They will not need to be jealous of each other, because they will be secure in knowing that Mom loves and values each one of them.

The bedtime ritual is a special time for mother and child. As each new child was born into our family, I had to be creative with the bedtime ritual so that each child still had special one-on-one time with me. I devised staggered bedtimes for my children, with each child having a fifteen-minute-later bedtime than the next youngest sibling. As they got older, that stretched to thirty minutes. To my children, this extra time seemed like a lot, and they appreciated the perk of getting to stay up later because they were older. Those fifteen minutes when they were young gave me the time to maintain the bedtime ritual with each child, starting with the youngest. My children always knew that no matter what else had happened that day, they would have that special one-on-one time with me at bedtime, and my attention would be solely on them.

I had started the staggered bedtimes with the first two children, and then baby number three came along. Of course, babies do not have bedtimes yet as newborns; they are not on a schedule yet. Since Mary Kate also had colic, she was often crying as Meghan and Matthew were going to bed. One night, I was sitting in the rocking chair in the den, consoling Mary Kate. Matthew, not quite three years old, was in his bed, chin propped on his hands, peeking into the den, and I could see he had a question. I went into his room to ask him what he was thinking. He asked, "Mommy, why do only the girls get to stay up later?"

In his mind, he was the boy with an earlier bedtime while his older sister and younger sister were still up. Meghan had a later bedtime because of the staggered bedtime and because she was the oldest; Mary Kate didn't yet have a bedtime since she was an infant. I explained this to him, and he did come to understand. I helped him to see that once Mary Kate was past the baby stage, she would have a bedtime, and it would be earlier than his since he was older. He was excited to think about that.

A wonderful way to work in alone time is solo outings with your children. It might just be that you are running an errand, and you take one of your children with you. That time in the car, running the errand together, is great for bonding and provides solo time between one child and one parent. You might create a mother-son or mother-daughter "date night" schedule, rotating between each child on a weekly schedule, monthly schedule, or whatever you can make work. Encourage your children's father to do the same. This is important for developing and nurturing sibling bonds. They will feel secure in their love with their parents.

While living in New England, we had friends who were the parents of four children. They created a way to have solo time with their children that really worked for them. It was a priority that once a month, the father would go out with one of their children for some time alone, and the mom would go out on an outing with one of the children as well. With two parents and four children, that meant a lot of activities. But it did not have to be anything extravagant, just an opportunity to make sure that each of those children felt secure and loved by having that time alone with each parent. If there was something that a child wanted to talk about, he or she had private time with a parent to do that.

When I was a little girl, there were a lot of changes after my mom died. My dad married again when I was four, and I became part of a blended family. With five kids, it was hard to find time alone with my new mom. I wanted that time with her so badly and felt I needed it. I would say to her, "Mommy, if you have to go pick up Paul [my older brother] from work, can you wake me up so I can ride in the car with you?"

She honored that. Even if it was a school night, she knew I really needed that time, especially after having just lost my mom and immediately having a blended family with extra siblings. She recognized my need to have time with just her. She would wake me up and let me ride with her. To this day, those memories of riding with her in the car at night, just the two of us, with the lights from other cars twinkling as we rode, are some of my favorite childhood memories.

When children are secure in their love from their parents, they will have stronger bonds with their siblings. If they are secure in their parents' love, they do not need to be jealous of each other. They will think, *I can love my siblings since they are not taking my mom's love away from me. I can love my siblings because my mom loves me for who I am, and it does not matter that my sibling is different.*

Dangers of Comparing

Never, never, never compare your children. There is nothing more detrimental to a sibling bond than playing favorites and comparing your children. Your children recognize it for what it is, and it makes them feel bad about themselves. When you compare your children, it sets up an unhealthy competition between them since they feel they must compete with each other for your affection. That is not the message you want to send to your children.

Your children should never be in competition for your love, because you should love all of them unconditionally for who they are. If they are competing with each other for your love, they feel they have to bring each other down to give themselves the edge. They will feel they have to make the other one look bad in your eyes in order to look better themselves.

Comparing children damages their relationships with their parents and their siblings. When you play favorites with your children, everyone in the family suffers. It is detrimental to the parents, to the child who is not favored, and to the child who is favored. The favored child will recognize that he or she is favored over another, and that will give the child a skewed view of his or her place in the family. Comparing and favoring are not healthy ways to raise children.

When you think about your children, if there is one whom you feel you are leaning toward or siding with, start working to stop that favoritism. Think of the positives that each child has and brings to your family. Reflect on each child's strengths, talents, and gifts.

Growing up, I did feel favoritism, that other siblings were favored over me. I was determined not to do that with my own children. Raising my kids, I would do a self-check and ask myself if there was one I favored over the other. I appreciated that all of my children were different; they were each unique and not at all like each other. I never felt that one pulled on my heartstrings more than the others. They have pulled on my heartstrings differently and uniquely, but never did one pull more strongly than another.

Do that check periodically so you can keep your interactions fair and loving to all. Ask yourself, *Is there a child that I am favoring more than others?* Ask other people close to you, "Do you notice that I am ever comparing or favoring one child over another?" Even when you do not intentionally favor a child or are not aware that you do it, you might hear back, "Yeah, recently I noticed Tilly is being favored whenever there is disagreement between her and her brother."

You can even check in with your children because they will tell you if they feel like somebody is getting something that they are not. You can help them be comfortable talking about that. It is a perfect opportunity to correct unintentional favoring and comparing and get back on the right track with appreciating all of your children for the unique beings they are.

When I was growing up, my little sister was such a cutie. She was a doll with a round little face, chubby little cheeks, curly brown hair, and big brown eyes. I would be out with my grandparents and my little sister, and people would stop and gush, "What a cute little girl! She has such beautiful brown eyes!"

I was three and a half years older and a bit more awkward-looking, and my grandmother would make the point of saying, "Oh yes, she is so cute! And doesn't her sister have the most gorgeous red hair and cute little freckles? Both of my granddaughters are so special!" In those moments, my grandmother would always include me, so I never really recognized that the person was complimenting only my little sister. I never felt jealous of my sister's looks. My grandmother made a point of making me feel just as treasured and just as loved.

Many times while growing up I would hear, "Why don't you do this like your sister or your brother?" I know that the intention was not to make me feel bad. However, even though that was not the intention, in those moments, I felt like I was not as special or loved.

Be very careful about what you say and how you say it when you are saying things about a sibling. Be mindful of not giving undue praise to one while the other is left to feel less than special. It is okay to praise your children when they are doing something good individually. Each child should be encouraged to shine individually and in his or her own unique way, but be careful that you do not make it appear as though one child is loved or favored more by giving that child unfair advantages. Spread out the praise so over the course of time, everyone will feel equally praised, appreciated, and loved.

Sibling bonds flourish when your children are secure in their love from their parents. Help your children feel so secure that they do not need to take anything away from a sibling in order to be more loved by their parents. As a mom, you have the greatest impact and influence in creating sibling bonds.

Friends for Life

One benefit of creating those sibling bonds is that you are setting your children up to be friends for a lifetime. When I was in my early twenties and first having my children, I thought about wanting to make sure they had each other long after their father and I had passed. Only they would share the same history as a family. When my children would get angry at each other or complain about each other, I would tell them, just as my great-grandmother had told her children, "The day is going to come when Mom and Dad won't be here anymore. All the experiences that you have had, the shared memories of your childhood—the only ones who will remember those special family moments will be your siblings. It is important to treasure your relationships with your siblings."

Growing up, my children were very close. They were a tight-knit group, but that does not mean they did not argue. Siblings argue and have disagreements; that is a part of all relationships. My children were close when they were all at home, and they still are close today.

When my son was applying to medical school several years ago, the first two years he tried, he was not accepted. My daughters both reacted similarly. "Why isn't Matthew getting accepted into medical school? Don't they see how intelligent and exceptional he is? Why don't they see what a great doctor he would be and what a difference he would make in the lives of his patients?"

My daughters were not relishing in the unfulfilled dreams of their brother. The exact opposite was true. Instead, they were incensed that others were not seeing the wonderful qualities in their brother that they knew were there. They were backing him and supporting him all the way.

When Mary Kate was deciding her potential career path, working toward her bachelor's degree, and making the decision of what degree she wanted, Matthew recognized her love of biology. He tried to encourage her to try for medical school herself. He did not once think, *That is my thing! I'm the one who will be the doctor. I'm the one who is going to take that path!* He wanted her to follow that path too. He recognized that she could excel at medicine, and he wanted her to achieve that if that was what she wanted.

My children have shared graduations and other good things with each other, and they have shared their challenges and helped each other through those challenges. They have been friends for each other, and even though they are not geographically close now, they are still close in communication. When there is some good news they want to share or something that they need to talk through with someone, they talk to each other. They know that their siblings will love them and have their back. They know that their siblings will not be jealous of them or send them in a wrong direction to make themselves look better.

If you ask any of my children who their best friends are, they will say that their siblings are. Meghan told me that a friend asked her once how she could think of her siblings as her best friends. She answered, "They just are. They are there for me, looking out for me. They want me to achieve my goals, and they help me when I need somebody to talk through difficulties with."

Through the years, many of my children's friends have told them that they wished they had sibling relationships like my children have since they themselves were not that close to their siblings. Sibling bonds are a gift that you give your children when you encourage and nurture those sibling relationships.

Do Not Kid Yourself—They Know

If you have a favorite among your children and you are thinking, *I do favor one child, but my other children do not know that,* trust me—they know. Children are very intuitive and pick up on things even when that is not your intent. I knew who the favorites were when I was growing up.

When we moved the summer before I entered seventh grade, there were three bedrooms in our new home and three children. It was time to pick bedrooms, and I was so excited. When it was over, my sister had the biggest room, my brother had a room similar in size to hers but in a better spot, and my room was tiny. I don't think the room was even meant to be a bedroom given its small size.

I was sad and wondered why I was getting this tiny little room as a seventh grader and my fourth-grade sister had the largest room. My parents explained their reasoning: my sister needed the room closest to my parents, and my brother needed a room large enough to keep the weights he and my dad used. No matter what explanation they gave, I couldn't help feeling less loved than my siblings.

My parents today think back on that and realize things should have been handled differently. They did not want or intend to make me feel bad, but in my mind, each parent had a favorite, and I was the odd child out. With a little discussion, the rooms could have been worked out with a more equitable distribution, which everyone realizes now.

If you are favoring a child, think about what you are doing to create that favoritism. Think about the unique and positive traits that each of your children has and be mindful of the interactions with all of your children. If there is a child you are favoring, take conscious steps to minimize the favoritism.

If there are children who are feeling less valued and disfavored, then make sure there is more equality in the way decisions are made so that you can create those sibling bonds. Once that jealousy is removed, the competition is removed, and you will be well on the way to your children feeling close to each other and having positive sibling bonds. In my own reality, I work very hard to make sure that no child ever feels favored over another.

Raising my children, I wanted to ensure that if my children were ever asked who my favorite was, they would respond that I did not have a favorite. Either that, or they would *all* feel like they were my favorite. Either one would be fine with me, as long as my children never felt that there was favoritism in our family that resulted in them getting the short end of the stick.

Mediating Fights

One place where you can get into trouble showing favoritism is when your children are having disagreements and you intervene. Sometimes it is easier to come in and settle the disagreement for them. Remember the saying that the squeaky wheel gets the grease? Sometimes moms will just side with a particular child because he or she is the loudest one, just to end it and be done with the noise and fighting.

You are not helping your children when you do this. First, you are not helping them strengthen their sibling bonds, and second, you are getting into the position of choosing sides. When that happens, you look like you are choosing a favorite. As much as you can, allow them to settle their own disagreements as long as no one is getting hurt. This is empowering, and it is a learning experience in working through things. It is a life skill to learn how to settle disagreements without getting physical about it.

When you do have to intervene because no progress is being made, help them get to the resolution. Give each child an opportunity to tell you what is going on and what the argument is about. Let one child speak, and then give the other child equal opportunity to voice his or her concern or how that child perceives the problem. Make the children listen to each other as one speaks and the other listens.

Do not take sides. You can reiterate what you heard one child say to the other, but do not take sides. Then you can ask them how they think they could settle this, what they could each do to help one another compromise on the situation, or whether there is something they would be okay allowing their sibling to get out of the situation. Help them reach that resolution without taking sides and without telling them what the resolution is going to be.

Sibling Support

As a mom, you are the center of your family, and you need to look out constantly for your family and create a positive family dynamic. Families support each other; that is what families are all about. Siblings are a very important part of the family, and they need to support each other.

When I was raising my children and they were involved in different things, we created that idea of sibling support and family support from the very beginning. If my children were involved in extracurricular activities—maybe they had a game or performance—we went as a family to support that child. That was not just special for the child playing or performing; it was special for the whole family as a unit, supporting one another and growing as a family. The next time that another sibling did something, we were all there for that sibling as well.

From the beginning, instill in your children that they need to support each other. My children support one another today and look at each other as best friends. This started from those earliest moments of supporting each other in their sports teams, in their play performances, and with their music performances.

As adults, they agreed that they would attend each other's first college graduation, for their bachelor's degrees, and each other's last, as they all went on to advanced degrees. When Meghan earned her education specialist degree in 2012, we were all in attendance, siblings included, to show our support and family pride.

Even with their own busy lives, my children have made an effort to be there for each other because they want to support each other. That was not something that we, as parents, had set up. It was an agreement that our children made with each other.

When Mary Kate graduated from college in 2013 with her bachelor's degree, Matthew was in the middle of medical school, an intense commitment. He was one week away from final exams for that semester, trying to do his best on everything because he was working toward a competitive residency. Our children had made their agreement years before, and he was going to honor it and be there for his sister.

As we sat in the audience waiting for the graduation ceremony to begin, Matthew was in his seat, note cards in hand, making use of every spare minute to study for his exam before the ceremony started. Beside him was his older sister, who was helping him study by quizzing him on the information on his note cards. What a powerful moment for me as a mom. On that day, Mary Kate graduated with her bachelor's degree with her siblings both in attendance, as they had promised. Even though Matthew had a very important exam a few days later, he was there, and Meghan was helping him to be there, sitting in the pew and spending all that waiting time helping him study.

When Matthew had his white coat ceremony to kick off the start of his second year in medical school, his sisters were there. When he had his match day ceremony which revealed where he had matched for medical residency, his sisters were there. These were not ceremonies that my daughters had to attend; they were not part of the first and last graduation agreement. But they recognized that my son had worked so hard for these for a long time, and they made the extra effort to be there, take part in the celebrations, and support their brother.

When Mary Kate graduated with her master's degree in 2015, her siblings were there with my husband and me, cheering her on and celebrating as a family. As Matthew's anticipated graduation from medical school in 2016 approaches, his sisters are well aware of the date. Just as they supported his efforts to get into medical school, they will be supporting him as he becomes a doctor.

My children were supportive of each other throughout childhood and are still supportive of each other today because they were raised to be supportive of each other. They are genuinely happy for each other's accomplishments. As you are raising your children, instill in them the need to bond and support each other as a family and as siblings so that the bond will carry on through their lifetimes.

Ways to Encourage

Throughout this chapter, you have read about the different ways that you can create and nurture those sibling bonds. My mom had her own way of doing that when she was raising my sister and me. My sister and I might have been out all day playing with our friends before being called in for dinner. If it was still light outside after dinner, we were allowed to go back out and play, but not with our friends. After dinner, my sister and I were allowed to play only with each other in the backyard, where we had a fabulous setup with a swing set and our toys. We loved that backyard and all it had to offer. Even though sometimes we could hear our friends up the street and might want to go back and join the fun, my sister and I had that bonding time that today, as adults, we wouldn't trade for anything. We had that time together to bond and play, just the two of us.

Family vacations are another opportunity to bond. We did not have a lot of extra money while raising our children. I chose to be a stay-at-home mom, and of course, that was a sacrifice that my husband and I both were willing to make. Because we were living on one income, our vacations were often scaled down. They were still such a bonding experience for my children, though, not just the long car rides we took but also that time to be together as a family.

When we lived in Georgia and in Florida, we were close to Disney World, so going there was not an extravagant vacation. We did not have to factor in all the usual transportation costs. It might be another long car ride, but it was something we could certainly afford to do.

On one of those trips, we were all very tired. We had enjoyed a whole day at Magic Kingdom and had just gotten back to the hotel, and Matthew and Mary Kate were still raring to go. They wanted to go back and ride more rides. They were young teenagers at that time, and my son said, "I want to go back and ride Space Mountain some more."

Matthew and Mary Kate decided that they would take the monorail back to Space Mountain. They wanted to get in as many more rides as they could before the end of the evening. I was thrilled that they were eager to share that time together, just the two of them.

A few years ago, as my children entered young adulthood, we decided to take a family cruise. They were all busy in their own lives with school and jobs, yet they cleared their schedules so that we could all share that family time together. We arranged for the three of them to share a room separate from their dad and me. We wanted to give them the time at night to catch up and have that same bonding time they'd had as children. As a mom, I know that time is priceless.

When we were raising our children, we created family movie nights. Either Friday or Saturday night, my children would choose a movie they all wanted to see, get the snacks ready, and crowd around the TV to share that time and watch a movie together. I cherished those moments, listening to the laughter and whispered conversations as the movie played in the background.

Nurture those bonds between your children. They are each other's shared history. Keep those sibling bonds strong; it is a lifelong gift you can give your children.

Chapter Four
The Gift of Rules, Structure, and Discipline

Discipline is helping a child solve a problem.
Punishment is making a child suffer for
having a problem. To raise problem solvers,
focus on solutions not retribution.
—L. R. Knost

Call from Meghan

When we were living in Iowa, I drove to the grocery store one day to pick up meat for dinner. My daughter called as I was stepping out of the car in the parking lot and said, "Mom, I just want to thank you for all of the rules you had for us when we were growing up and the way you disciplined us when we needed it."

Meghan was twenty-one years old at the time, and I was struck by how mature she sounded in that moment. That is a call most moms think they will never receive. We raise our children day in and day out, but we do not expect our children to recognize or thank us for that. She had been sitting around talking with some of her friends and was shocked at some of the negative experiences they had lived through and were sharing

77

with her. What struck my daughter the most was that these friends had not been raised with structure, rules, or discipline in their lives.

Meghan said to me, "I am so thankful that you had those rules in place. Now I know why you wanted to know where we were and who we were with and why you wanted us home by a set time. There were rules in place because you wanted to be sure we would not get in situations that could turn out badly for us. Thank you for loving us enough to do that."

In that moment, I could not have been more proud of her. As moms, we do not raise our children with the idea that someday they will thank us. We do it because we love our children and want to do the best that we can for them. How wonderful it is when your child recognizes that. Your children may never tell you, but I do believe that they always recognize when you have loved them with their best interests at heart.

Being the Bad Guy

One of the hardest things in parenting, but a very necessary thing, is to have in place rules, structure, and discipline. The rewards for raising children are not instant. It takes years of raising your children before you can see how the effort is even turning out. It is a life's work for moms. You just do the best that you can to raise your children right, with love always as the motivator. You want your children to be functioning members of society who add positivity to the world. To that end, you must be their parent and not their friend. Your children may have plenty of friends, but they do not have anybody else who will be their mom. You are their mom; treasure that role. It is so much better than being their friend.

Several years ago, I was getting a pedicure when the technician began talking to me about her fifteen-year-old daughter. As we were sharing mom stories, she admitted to me that she had made a big mistake with her daughter. She told me, "I thought when my daughter became a teenager, I needed to be her friend. I thought we would have a better relationship if I wasn't always having to enforce rules and discipline her."

Unfortunately, that decision had such a bad outcome. Her daughter started hanging with the wrong crowd, getting into trouble, and being disrespectful, and the list goes on. The daughter got into trouble because the mom was not being her mom; she was trying to be her friend. The technician explained that now she was trying to change back to behaving like a mom, and it was not easy. She knew that she needed to do this but lamented that it was a difficult process. The mom had come to the right realization. I knew that they could not be friends; that girl needed a mom. I was glad that this mom had begun turning things around before things got worse for her daughter. You can have a wonderful relationship with your child, but that relationship must be mom-to-child, not friend-to-friend.

I think about the movie *Mean Girls* starring Lindsay Lohan in the lead role. If you have seen the movie, you know that Regina George, played by Rachel McAdams, has a mother who wants to be her friend. The mom, played by Amy Poehler, is free and easy with her daughter. The daughter gets the master bedroom and has free rein with drinking, boys, and other inappropriate behaviors. The mom so wants to be accepted as her child's friend that she gives up her authority to be a friend to her daughter instead. If you have seen the movie, you know how that turns out.

Several years ago, I had a student whose parents had split up. He was being raised by his mother, and she had taken on the idea that being a friend to her son was the best way to raise him. She did not hold her child accountable for his behavior, and that behavior carried over into my classroom. I recognized right away that there was no authority figure at home. Nobody was disciplining, setting rules for, or creating structure for this child. It was not in his best interest, and it was causing him to get into trouble at school.

It was a very unhealthy situation, and before long, the student's dad recognized that the mom was not being a parent. The dad intervened and arranged for the son to live with him. In the classroom, I saw an immediate turnaround for the student when he was in a household where there were rules, structure, and discipline. He was not just with his mother, who only wanted to be his friend; he was living with a father who was an authority figure.

Your child will have many friends in life but likely only one mom. Treasure that role for the very special one that it is. Don't give it away by trying to befriend your child.

From the Eyes of an Educator

As an educator, I have taught many students and have found that what manifests in the classroom is often a window into what is going on at home. I have learned from the children I have taught that kids crave rules, structure, and discipline, even if they may not let you know this. They will roll their eyes, complain, and say unkind things and may even sigh as they are walking away from you after you have put a rule in place that they don't like or agree with. As they do all those things, though, they recognize that someone cares enough to put rules in place, and they appreciate that.

They know that they need to have rules, structure, and discipline. Even when they are testing the limits and pushing back against them, they know that they need these things. When parents put rules and structure in place, children recognize that their parents do love them.

Kids need structure to survive in the real world. When they get into school settings and life, where they are trying to hold down jobs, working toward college, or maybe working toward a particular achievement, they will encounter structure, rules, and discipline. They will learn quickly that you cannot always do what you want to do.

There are laws and rules in life. There is structure in life. There will be consequences if you do not do the right thing. It is your job to put those rules, structure, and discipline in place. You are giving your children the experience of learning to live within that framework. The real world will not be a shock to them because they will be used to rules, structure, and discipline.

Not Easy to Parent with Rules and Structure

It is not easy to parent children with rules, structure, and discipline; it requires a lot of time and energy. If you were to be a mom who raises her children without enforcing rules, creating structure, or instilling discipline, your children would do whatever they want, and you would just be a bystander. Moms can't just be bystanders.

If you do not have rules, structure, and discipline, then you are not really parenting your children. You are not being the mom they need. Rules, structure, and discipline teach your children that they must follow guidelines, work within boundaries, and take responsibility for their actions. Lax parenting allows your children to do what they want, with no rules to follow, no structure in their day, and no discipline when they misbehave. Children in these situations have free rein and do not worry about parents imposing consequences if they do something wrong.

If there are no rules, structure, or discipline, there is no wrong. Proper behavior expectations do not exist. Lax parenting leads to children who are not ready to survive in the real world. Lax parenting leads to children who will get themselves into situations that they are not ready for.

Children raised without rules, structure, and discipline often travel down a path that their parents do not want them to follow. They often make poor decisions, get in with the wrong crowd, or put themselves in dangerous situations. These children sometimes have to pay hefty consequences for the choices they have made.

When your children are babies, some of the structure that you have to put in place relates to things such as bottles, pacifiers, tantrums, and sleeping. Even then, when they are very little, you have to put structure and discipline in place. By starting then, you will be practicing for the years ahead.

When my first daughter was born, I knew I did not want her to be a thumb-sucker, so I decided right away that I would use the pacifier. I thought it would be easier to break the pacifier habit when the time came since a pacifier can easily be taken away. A thumb is always attached! I read in a baby book that babies do not need pacifiers after about six months old. Since Meghan had already reached that age, I decided to start breaking the habit. I knew that at six months, she did not have an emotional attachment to it and would not really fight against it. I found other ways to soothe her that took the place of sucking on a pacifier. The transition was an easy one.

Several months later, I took Meghan to the doctor for her checkup a few days after her first birthday. I asked the doctor, "At what age should I start weaning her off the bottle?"

He looked at me and said, "Every moment that you wait past one year old will just make it that much harder."

I looked at my daughter, quite certain she was comprehending, and said, "Well, today I guess we are going home and starting to wean you off that bottle!"

Despite my first-time mommy worries, it was actually a pretty easy thing to do. She was not old enough to have a strong desire for it, and in a couple of days, she was off the bottle and drinking exclusively from a cup. It was no big deal.

I have seen children who are three, four, and even five years old with pacifiers and bottles, and it makes me think that either the parents just do not want to deal with the frustration, or perhaps the parents think they are harming their child if they take the pacifier or bottle away because the child will be sad.

Either way, even though it may be a little inconvenient and the parents may have to deal with some hardship in the beginning, breaking the habit will be better for the child. Since the child doesn't really need it anymore after a certain age, by providing some structure, the parent will prevent the pacifier or bottle from becoming a crutch.

As moms, we all know that we learn on that first child, and my case was no different. When Meghan was several months old, she was still waking up many times throughout the night and had a hard time putting herself back to sleep. I was sharing my concern with a friend whose daughter had recently started sleeping through the night. She told me about a book by Dr. Richard Ferber, which had just been published, that she had used to get her daughter to sleep through the night. I went out that day, bought the book, read it from cover to cover, reviewed the plan with my husband, and put the plan into play.

At first, it was heart-wrenching. We would put Meghan to bed and close the door, and then the crying would begin. We followed the plan, allowing her to cry briefly before going in to soothe her without picking her up and then leaving the room once more. We continued the protocol Dr. Ferber suggested in his book, and within a week, Meghan was sleeping through the night. She became such a good sleeper that even as a baby, we could put her to bed at seven o'clock at night, and she would sleep until seven the next morning. Even though it was difficult and took time and effort, it was a structure we needed to put in place for her best interest.

As a mom, learn to embrace the notion that if your kids do not hate you at least once in a while, then you are not doing your job. In my own experience, I have found that to be true. If you are always trying to be popular in your children's eyes, wanting them to like you at every moment, then you are not being the mom they need you to be.

You have to accept that sometimes your kids are going to hate you and tell you that you are too strict or that their friends get to do something you don't allow them to do. If you are a mom who raises your children with rules, structure, and discipline, you will likely hear that more than once. If the rules, structure, and discipline are coming from a place of love and a place of looking out for their best interests, embrace this!

When raising my children, I kept a poem posted on my refrigerator that was titled "I Had the Meanest Mother in the World," and I would read that poem for strength when my kids "hated" me or bristled at my rules. In essence, the poem was about "the meanest mother" who had rules, structure, and discipline in place for her children and how wonderful they turned out because of her. Don't be afraid for your kids to "hate" you every once in a while.

Think about the Big Picture

When you are implementing rules, structure, and discipline in your own household, think about the big picture. What is it ultimately that you are trying to achieve by having this rule, structuring things in this way, or disciplining in that way? The big picture is particularly important when it comes to rules. If the rule is in place simply to have a rule, it probably will not be helpful to your children. The rules should be in place because they will help your child become a better person. Implementing rules just to have rules will be counterproductive. Rules to help your children learn a lesson, become responsible, or develop strong values will help them grow into contributing members of society. If your rules are in place to accomplish goals such as these, then you know that the rules are serving a positive function in your child's life.

Rules are necessary and beneficial in raising children, but too many rules can backfire. If you are too overprotective, that will be counterproductive and won't produce the results you want. Rules should be in place to protect your children, to teach them responsibility and compassion, and to help them be the best that they can be. Avoid creating a situation where there are so many rules that your children have no freedoms at all. If they cannot even breathe without there being some rule about it, that will backfire. Rules should have value.

Once the rules have been set, communicate them clearly and enforce them. Nothing is worse than setting a rule, communicating that rule, and then never enforcing that rule. Children pick up on it very quickly when the rules are not enforced. If a rule is not enforced, it stops being a rule.

If you are setting rules for valuable reasons, then be prepared to discipline your children if the rules are not followed. For instance, let's say you put a rule in place about expectations for grades. If your child is not spending enough time on homework, and you notice that your child's grades are slipping because of it, intervene and put a plan in place to help him study more so his grades will improve. That is where the discipline will come in.

The discipline should clearly relate to the rule that has been broken. You might say, "Your grades are slipping, and I have noticed you are not spending enough time on homework. From now until the end of the grading period, you will not be allowed to watch television on school nights until I see an improvement in your grades. Once your grades improve, you will earn back one hour of TV on school nights after homework is completed. If after the grading period you have shown that you have learned to prioritize your schoolwork, we can discuss how to proceed in the next grading period and make any adjustments we think are appropriate."

When I was raising my children, I started to see that technology was becoming a bit too important, and reading was no longer the go-to leisure activity. My children were rushing to finish their homework so they could get on their computers, TVs, and phones. I knew I needed to address the problem immediately. I instituted "no-technology time" on school nights between 4:00 and 6:00 p.m., which gave my children time to get a snack and maybe watch a quick show or play a quick video game when they got home from school. Then it was total blackout of technology from 4:00 to 6:00 p.m., which meant no video games, no television, no phones, no technology at all. That was the time for doing homework, and even if they finished their homework before six, they were not allowed to spend time with their technology until no-technology time was over. That prevented them from rushing through homework just so they could spend time with technology, and it also helped them rediscover their love of reading and playing outside.

My children quickly learned that no matter what, they could not turn that technology back on until after six. Since six o'clock was usually dinnertime, they were not back on technology until closer to seven o'clock because dinner was always spent as a family around the table. After dinner, my children had dishes to load in the dishwasher, tables to wipe down, and pots to clean, and then if they wanted to turn on technology, they could.

If you see that there is a need for a rule or structure, set a plan in place and make sure you have done everything you can to make it successful. Communicate what the rule is, why it is being put in place, and what you hope the outcome will be. Remind your children that if they do not follow the rule, they will be disciplined. Otherwise, a rule not enforced is no longer a rule.

Determining Rules That Will Work for You

When creating rules and structure in your own family, think about what is important to you. What fits with your family values and your morals? The rules that are important to me for my family and the ones that are important to your best friend for her family are not necessarily the best rules for you to put in place for your family. Think about what meshes with your family and what you want to achieve value-wise as you are determining what those rules will be.

When I was raising my children, I did not want them to experience things until I thought they were mature enough for the experiences. When it came to movies, my children did not watch PG-13 movies until they were thirteen years old. For many parents, movie ratings are not a big deal, but to me, the issue was very important. That meant that if my child was invited to a friend's house for a sleepover and a movie was going to be shown, I had to do my duty as a mom and call the other mom to ask what movies would be shown. If the kids were going to watch a PG-13 movie, then I would let the parent know that I was not comfortable with my child seeing a PG-13 movie, and we would work around it. That might mean my child would show up later to the sleepover. I never wanted the hostess to feel she had to rearrange her plans. At the same time, I had to do what I felt was right for my child.

When my children were young, many of the most popular shows of the day were also shows that I felt were inappropriate, and my children were not allowed to watch them. Even though their friends might be watching a certain show, if I felt it was inappropriate, then my children were not going to watch that show. I did not want my children exposed to some of the situations, dialogue, and graphic content of those TV shows until I felt they were mature enough to handle it. Other activities were much better uses of their time.

As for raising daughters, in my mind there was no reason for them to be wearing makeup before they were in high school. Other people feel that makeup at younger ages is fine, and everyone has a right to his or her opinion. As a mom, you have to do what works for your family, just as I did with mine. I did not want my daughters to feel like they needed to wear makeup to be pretty or popular or accepted. They were beautiful to me as they were, and I wanted them to learn they were beautiful without makeup. They were not dating at that age either, which is often what drives young ladies to want to wear makeup. Because they were made to hold off on wearing makeup until high school, my daughters felt like it was an earned rite of passage when they did reach high school.

When they got to high school, I was still there to remind them to use only light eye shadow, a little bit of blush, and some lip gloss. I didn't want them to think wearing makeup meant layering it on like they were about to go onstage. We had conversations about how to properly use makeup so that it enhanced their natural beauty rather than covering it up.

My girls are adults now, and I had not thought about makeup rules in quite a while until about a year ago, when Mary Kate said, "If I ever have a daughter, I am going to have that same makeup rule you had with Meghan and me. You know what? I did not *need* to be wearing makeup in middle school."

Through all those moments when my daughters were rolling their eyes, telling me that all their friends were wearing makeup and that I was being unfair, I held my ground because I was thinking of the big picture. My daughters look back on it now and recognize that the rule was in place for the right reasons. They recognize the value and do appreciate that I loved them enough to have that rule.

Another rule that was important to me had to do with dating. We did not allow our children, our daughters or our son, to solo date until they were sixteen years old. They could go out on group dates before sixteen, and before that they were allowed to do things with friends, both boys and girls, with proper supervision. But a solo date, just one guy and one girl, was not allowed until they were sixteen years old. This too had to do with my view that I did not want my children to experience something that they were not mature enough to handle.

A driving force behind many of the rules I put in place with my children was that I wanted them to enjoy being young. In today's society, there is such a push for our kids to grow up too fast, and I wanted to protect my children's right to be children. I knew they would not get the chance to go back and have that childhood again. We need to respect their childhoods and allow our children the time to enjoy being young.

Teach your children to have respect for themselves and to be confident enough to make the right decisions even when others around them are making the wrong ones. As a mom, you are there to help your children avoid situations in which they will have to make choices where the impact of a wrong choice could be greater than they are ready to deal with. Help your children understand consequences and recognize those situations where the results could be detrimental if they make the wrong choice.

My children still remind me about how they were not allowed to watch a lot of television when they were little. They were encouraged to do other things—play outside, play with neighborhood friends, take a walk as a family, make arts and crafts, create projects, read, or do anything appropriate other than watching television. They recognize now how valuable that was for them. They make comments about seeing children who have nothing of importance in their lives except technology, and they are glad I had that rule in place. In the end, put rules in place that will benefit your children in the long run. The whole point of rules is that you are looking out for your children's best interests.

What If They Rebel?

Trust me, your children will rebel. They will rebel against your rules and structure. It will happen, and when it does, make sure you have a response ready. For example, you might hear, "Why won't you let me do that? Sarah gets to do it!"

When I heard such questions from my children, I would respond, "I am not Sarah's mom. If I were Sarah's mom, she would not be allowed to do this either." Or I might respond, "I have to do what I think is right for you. This is what I feel is right because at the end of the day, I am looking out for your best interests." In difficult situations, I would even remind them of my important role in their lives by saying, "It is my job to make sure you get to heaven."

Be prepared. Your children will rebel against the rules. It is natural and normal for them to do that. You just need to be ready to respond appropriately to the rebellion. Remember that the ultimate goal as a mom is to raise children who are thoughtful, independent, and responsible members of society.

As a mom, you are changing the world every day as you raise your children. The child whom you raise may someday be the leader of a corporation, the leader of a community, the leader of a church, or the leader of a state or our country. Prepare your children and make sure that they are good people by raising them to be kind, thoughtful, independent, successful, compassionate, and responsible individuals.

Life skills are first learned at home. If you are not teaching your children those life skills, you are sending them out into the world without everything they need to be successful. Being a mom is hard work, but at the same time, it is so very rewarding. God gives us these children to mold and raise, making sure they are learning the right way and making good choices for themselves and the world. Put rules and structure in place and then hold your children accountable.

If you put the rules and structure in place but do not make sure your children are accountable, the rules and structure do not mean anything. You have to hold them accountable because that is how they learn to function in the real world. If your children make a mistake in the real world, they will be held accountable. If they break a rule, they must be disciplined fairly and without anger. When anger comes into play after children break the rules, it is easy to overreact and go too far. You may find it necessary to take a step back and wait a few minutes before you come in to discipline. You can certainly tell your child that you need to think about this for a few minutes and then will come back to talk about the consequence. The entire point of discipline is for the child to learn right from wrong. It is not about harming the child.

Natural Consequences

One of the best ways to discipline your child is to let natural consequences take over. Natural consequences are the consequences imposed by nature, society, or someone other than the parents. If your child forgets her mittens and her hands are cold at recess, that is a natural consequence. She will remember the next day to take her mittens because her cold hands at recess made her uncomfortable. Mom did not impose that consequence; nature did.

If your child forgets his homework and earns a zero, that is a natural consequence. The teacher is imposing what is a natural consequence because the homework was due, your child had a responsibility, and your child did not live up to that responsibility for the class. Next time homework is due, your child will remember that zero and think twice about forgetting the homework. If you put a plan in place to help your children remember something the next time, that will help. Do not, however, rescue them from the current consequence.

If a child refuses to eat dinner and later she gets hungry, that is a natural consequence. The next day when dinner is served, she will eat because she will remember how she felt the night before when her tummy was grumbling. One night without dinner will make your child hungry, but it will not cause her overall harm. She will learn not to refuse dinner. If you are not comfortable with that idea, then you might choose to remind your child that the meal on the table is what is being served for dinner and you are not making anything else. If she chooses to make something else, that is fine, as long as there are some parameters and you can ensure that she is making something healthy. You don't want to allow her to just head to the cookie jar.

If your child misses practice and the coach keeps him from playing in the game, that is a natural consequence. Your child will learn that if he wants to be on that field playing the game, he better get to practice. He will remember that sitting out and watching is not nearly as much fun as being in the game.

For natural consequences to be effective, allow those natural consequences to take place, and do not intervene on your child's behalf. We all hate to see our children uncomfortable or disappointed, so it can be difficult to let the natural consequences play out. When you are feeling the urge to intervene, step back and take a look at the big picture. What are you ultimately trying to achieve? If the goal is to help your children learn to be responsible, they will learn that much more quickly if you let the consequences play out. One game spent sitting on the bench is much easier for your child to take than being kicked off the team. One zero for missed homework is much easier for your child to overcome than five. As much as you can, rein in your urge to intervene, and allow those natural consequences to do their job.

When Mary Kate was learning to drive, we lived in a state that had graduated licensing. That meant drivers earned their driving privileges in steps. Each step required a certain number of hours behind the wheel, a specific number of supervised hours, and no traffic violations or accidents during that time before the driver could earn full privileges with no restrictions. If there were any infractions during the required time period, then the driver had to start all over at that level and could not graduate to the next level until the new time period was completed without any infractions or accidents.

When my daughter was just a month away from graduating to that last level of licensing, which would have given her full privileges with no restrictions, she got a speeding ticket. She did not tell us about the ticket right away because she knew we would require her to take responsibility, and she knew we would be disappointed. She wanted to figure everything out and get her paycheck from her part-time job before she told us. A few days later she said, "Mom, I got a speeding ticket. The cost is $200, and I have the money to pay for it."

My daughter knew already that we would not pay her speeding ticket; she was the one who had chosen to speed, and we would hold her accountable for that. Since she was in the graduated licensing system, the natural consequence imposed by society was that she was required to attend a meeting with a law enforcement officer and a parent. The police officer explained to Mary Kate that she would have to start all over at the current level and would not graduate to the next level until she had completed the required time—again without any accidents or infractions.

Mary Kate was disappointed. She was about to start her senior year of high school and still would not have full driving privileges, but we did not step in to rescue her. I went with her to the meeting and listened to the law enforcement officer explain the consequences of the speeding ticket. The natural consequences provided an important learning experience for Mary Kate. She knew she had made the choice to speed; she had to pay the ticket and start all over to obtain her full driving privileges. For the duration of that time period, she was a much more careful driver, and when the time was up, she finally graduated to a license with full privileges.

As critical as it is to allow natural consequences to happen, you *must* intervene if safety is an issue and *prevent* the natural consequences. If your child is going to step into the street and be hit by a car, you cannot let that happen. You must protect your child in instances such as this. However, if the natural consequence is simply a challenge, obstacle, frustration, or discomfort resulting from your child's choices, let the natural consequence play out.

Discipline versus Punishment

When natural consequences are not appropriate either because there are no natural consequences in place or because safety is an issue, then you have to step in and provide the discipline. Discipline should always be logical and appropriate. If your child forgets to pick up his toys, you might remind him to pick them up. If he still does not pick up his toys, then you take those toys away for a period of time. That is logical. If your child goes to a friend's house without permission, thus breaking a family rule, then an appropriate disciplinary action would be not allowing the child to go to that friend's house for a specified period of time. That is an appropriate discipline for the infraction.

When you step in to discipline, make sure that the discipline is logical and appropriate so that it means something to the child and she recognizes it as an opportunity to learn. The child has to recognize the connection between the discipline and the offense for it to be most effective—*I did not pick up my toys even though Mom reminded me.* You want them to understand the cause and effect. *I did not value picking up my toys, and now I do not get to play with them. I went to Sarah's house without permission, and now I cannot go to Sarah's house for a week.*

Time-outs work wonderfully with young children, even though it can sometimes be difficult to reason with them. By using time-outs, you will be teaching them at a young age that there are certain things they are not allowed to do. You will be teaching them that there are rules in place that must be abided by.

When enforcing time-out, the time-out should be an appropriate length. One minute per year of age is a good rule of thumb. Do not just put your children into time-out without letting them know why they are there and what the offense was. They must recognize that there is a reason for the time-out and understand clearly the rule that was broken. When time-out is over, ask for that apology and let your child know that you love her. Give her a hug or a kiss and remind her again that it was the behavior that was wrong; the child is still loved very much.

As your children get older, loss of privileges is an excellent way to appropriately and logically discipline your children. Several years ago, my friend's teenage daughter charged up the family's cell phone bill through frequent and lengthy phone calls. Unlimited plans were not yet available. My friend opened her cell phone bill and almost fainted when she saw the outrageous number next to "Amount due." My friend and her husband sat their daughter down, explained the unacceptability of her actions, and suspended her cell phone service for one month with one quick call to the phone company. Their daughter immediately learned the value of her cell phone. Every time she wanted to call a friend and couldn't, she was reminded again that her irresponsibility had caused her current predicament. When the month was over and she had her phone back, she had a new appreciation for it and a better understanding of how to use it responsibly.

Older children recognize loss of privileges as a disciplinary action connected to an offense. After Meghan got her driver's license, she hit our neighbor's mailbox. She came home and told us and was visibly upset about it. We told her that the first thing she had to do was go to the neighbor, explain what she had done, and offer to pay for the damage to the mailbox. That was number one. She had damaged someone else's property, and she was going to have to make amends. We were holding her accountable and asking her to face the music by telling the neighbor what she had done and by paying for the damage to the mailbox. Second, she had to pay for the damage to our car. The windshield was broken, and she had to cover the insurance deductible from the money she had been saving from her paychecks, which was sitting in the bank for just such emergencies.

When she explained everything to the neighbors, they appreciated her honesty so much that when they looked at their mailbox and saw only a small dent, they told her that she did not have to pay anything to repair it. She learned the importance of acknowledging her mistakes and taking responsibility for them. Of course, she still had to pay for the damage to our car, and she learned to pay more attention behind the wheel when she had to part with hard-earned money. That was logical and appropriate discipline.

As you are disciplining your children, be mindful of the difference between discipline and punishment. Discipline serves a purpose. Your children learn the consequences of their poor behavior or breaking of the rules. Appropriate discipline helps your children learn responsibility and promotes maturity.

Punishment, on the other hand, is hurtful and demeaning and serves no real purpose other than to frighten your child. It might stop your children in the moment, but they will not learn anything other than your physical power over them. They will learn that their mom can hurt them. That is not an appropriate message to send to your children.

Discipline is a positive thing and helps children learn the consequences of their behavior. That will serve them well in society. It is better that they have a few tears now because of being disciplined appropriately than have a jail cell later because they did not understand that poor behavior and law-breaking have consequences. Discipline is in their best interest; punishment is never of value. You should never physically hurt your children because they did something wrong; that is very detrimental to their well-being. Certainly discipline them, but do not punish them.

Avoid Spanking

If you are spanking your children, you are teaching them that physically hurting someone is the way to deal with an issue, and that is not a healthy message to send your children. You might have been raised in a generation where physical punishment and spanking were acceptable; that is how I was raised. My siblings and I knew that if we did something really, really wrong, there was going to be a belt taken to our backside. Bad behavior would result in physical consequences for that behavior.

Even when I was going to school, corporal punishment was okay. The principal had a paddle in his office, and if a student came in with a particular infraction, there were paddles on the behind for it. The number of paddles the student had to endure depended on the severity of the infraction.

If you were raised in an environment where spanking was the norm, it is easy for it to become the go-to method for dealing with your own children's poor behavior and rule breaking. If your children are fighting among themselves and hitting each other, how do you explain that it is not okay for them to hit each other if you are punishing them with spanking? Recognize that connection and think about all the other ways you can discipline your children that are more appropriate than spanking.

Some people are of the opinion that if you do not spank your children, then your children will be poorly behaved. Nothing could be farther from the truth. When Matthew and Mary Kate were four years and eighteen months, respectively, we were involved in a car accident. As I was returning from picking up Matthew from preschool, an elderly man ran a stop sign and broadsided us. Thank God my children were safely strapped in their car seats in the backseat.

Since my car was so damaged that it could not be driven, we had to call my husband to come pick us up. While we were waiting, the three of us sat in the back of the police car. The police officer was sitting in the front seat, filling out his report, and my children and I were talking among ourselves in the backseat. My children were sitting still, carrying on a quiet conversation with me, respectful of where they were. After several minutes, the police officer turned around and said, "Your children are so well behaved! I am very impressed!"

My children learned proper behavior, and I never spanked them. You too can raise properly behaved children without spanking them. As a matter of fact, they will actually be better behaved in the long run if you do not use spanking as the way to deal with their poor behavior. To be effective, discipline must relate to the infraction. Hitting, on the other hand, is an abusive power. How does hitting your children relate to the fact that they forgot to pick up their toys? Your children will not make a connection between the two.

Do not punish your children or spank them. You are stronger than that because you are a mom who loves her children. It takes more strength to choose appropriate discipline than to raise your hand to strike your child. Proper discipline will create a stronger bond with your children, and you will prove that you are someone for them to love and respect rather than fear.

When my husband and I married and began talking about children, we had a difference of opinion on how we were going to raise them when it came to discipline. I had grown up in environments where the common way to deal with significant misbehavior was physical punishment, and I was adamant that we were not going to do that with our children. I had also read enough child psychology books and articles to know that the tide was beginning to turn against spanking children. On the other hand, my husband did not think that there was anything wrong with spanking.

Luckily, my husband was receptive to my reasoning behind not wanting to spank our children. We were able to get on the same page about how we would discipline our children before we even had them. All three of our children were raised without being spanked. Our children were certainly disciplined when they broke rules; they had structure in place, but they were not spanked.

If you are spanking your children, and you do not know what else to do, think about some of the other options that I have detailed here in this chapter. As you review those options, you will begin to see how logical and appropriate they are. Your children will learn valuable lessons from those forms of discipline, and yet they will be disciplined in a loving and appropriate way.

Raise your children in such a way that others will feel confident that your children will behave when in their presence and in their homes. You do not want to visit the homes of your friends and family knowing that they are fearful that your children are going to misbehave. You do not want to visit a doctor's office and see the staff cringing when you walk through the door with your children. Raise your children to be properly behaved with rules, structure, and loving discipline so that when you take your children places, people will be in awe of their behavior.

You are the mom and the essence of love in your children's lives. When you show that you can raise well-behaved children without raising your hand to spank them, then you are a catalyst for others to rethink how they are disciplining their own children. When you raise your children with rules, structure, and discipline, you have given them a gift that will be a powerful asset to them throughout their lifetime.

Chapter Five
The Gift of Responsibility

The moment you take responsibility for
everything in your life is the moment you
can change anything in your life.
—Hal Elrod

Hand in Hand with Rules, Structure, and Discipline

Responsibility goes hand in hand with rules, structure, and discipline. When children are raised with limits and consequences, they learn responsibility. It is hard to know when your children are toddling around the house what they will need when they grow up. When they reach their teenage years and go on into adulthood, make sure they are prepared so they can be successful and responsible adults.

Your children are a blessing from God, and you probably don't always like to think about them growing up. It is hard to imagine that the children you love and are raising day in and day out, in whose well-being you are investing countless hours of time, will one day grow up and live lives of their own, on their own, but your children *will* grow up. They will grow up to be responsible adults or irresponsible ones, and the last thing any mom wants to do is add more adults into the world who are irresponsible. Raise responsible children so that they become responsible adults and make positive contributions to our world and society. The gift of responsibility gives them the foundation for success in life because in the real world we have to be responsible to be successful.

Chores around the House

Give your children chores to do around the house, and in order to teach responsibility, do not tie the chores to an allowance. Children benefit from recognizing that some chores are required of them because they are part of a family, and they are expected to contribute as part of that family. Responsibility does not always mean a monetary reward.

Even the youngest children can accomplish tasks such as making their beds. Three-year-olds can make their beds, and three is actually a great age to start delegating some appropriate chores. It is not difficult to pull up a sheet, blanket, and comforter, put a pillow on top, and be done. As part of their family responsibility, some appropriate chores for your children at varying ages might include taking out the trash, loading and unloading the dishwasher, cleaning their rooms, feeding pets, and even washing clothes.

When I was raising my children, when they got to be about the age of ten, I started letting them take over their laundry. I taught them how to sort clothes, choose the wash temperature, and add the right amount of detergent. I also taught them the different settings for the machines and how to choose the right ones for washing and drying and then how to fold clothes properly and put them away.

As your children grow, reassess what they are now capable of doing, and adjust the chores accordingly so that you teach them to be responsible for themselves. Why should they expect you to do things that they are more than capable of doing themselves? Empower your children with the knowledge of how to do those things on their own.

If your children have some chores that they do as their family contribution, you might want to designate additional chores that they can do for money. For example, let's say your child's set chores as part of his family responsibility are to clean his room weekly, feed and walk the dog, and make his bed daily. If he wants to earn some money, you might offer the options of cleaning windows, cleaning out the garage, helping set up for a garage sale, or cleaning out kitchen cabinets and separating and organizing the contents. Plenty of other things can fit the additional chore category too, such as washing the car, raking leaves, or whatever you deem appropriate. As long as there are chores that your children do strictly as part of their family responsibility, then additional chores can be given for extra money.

When I was raising my children, they started making their beds at three years old, and they actually were proud to be given the responsibility. It takes a little longer for a three-year-old, but I was not striving for perfection. If you give this chore to your little ones, remember to appreciate their efforts and remember that the bed does not have to look perfect. Making their beds teaches your children to keep things in order, and it is not a strenuous or difficult activity. Young children can pick up their own toys when playtime is over for the day. At first, you will need to help them so they learn where the toys belong when not in use.

As my children grew older, they had the responsibility of cleaning their rooms. Usually one day a week, on Saturday, I would clean the house. As I was cleaning the house, they would take responsibility for their own rooms. That meant they picked up, dusted, emptied the trash can, and vacuumed their rooms. The bathroom that my children shared was their responsibility to clean, but I gave them some authority over how to deal with it. I suggested maybe a rotating schedule regarding which child would clean it, or they could clean it together each time, dividing up the different chores such as cleaning the sink, cleaning the bathtub, and mopping the floor. They decided how they were going to do the job, but they understood it was their responsibility to keep the bathroom clean.

Your goal is to teach your children that picking up after themselves is their own responsibility; it is not Mommy's job to do that. Making beds and doing laundry are life skills, and at an appropriate age, they can learn these skills. Chores are meant to help them learn responsibility and set them up for success later in life.

Extracurricular Activities

If your resources allow, encourage your children to get involved in extracurricular activities, and even if resources are limited, some options exist that require little to no money to join. Many do require funds, so find what will work with your own budget and encourage those activities. Options for extracurricular activities include scouting, sports teams, band, chorus, church groups, and many other things that your child may choose to get involved with.

Extracurricular activities teach not only responsibility but also the value of being a team player, which is another critical life skill. When you are on the job after all, you are often working in a team environment. You can help your children choose which activities interest them and match the values you want to instill in them.

Once your children have selected the activities they will participate in, have a conversation about the expectations. When they have a practice or a meeting, they must go. They have made an obligation to that team or club, and they must follow through on that commitment. They must also give their best when they are participating because that is how they help the team or club. Being a part of a team or club teaches responsibility by teaching them to honor their commitments and contribute their best efforts.

Along the way, you might hear, "But I do not want to go to practice." Maybe your child has come home from school and is tired, or she thinks of all her homework and feels overwhelmed. That is a great opportunity to sit with your child and explain about her commitment to the team or group and how important it is to keep that commitment. "Let's sit down and figure out how you will get everything done that you need to do and still fulfill your commitment."

Take these opportunities to help your children learn time-management skills. Put all the things they have to do in an order so that they can get them all done—so that they can go to the practice or meeting and still get their homework done in a timely fashion and do it well. How many times do we as adults wake up and think, *Oh, I just do not feel like going to work today.* We still put our feet on the floor, get ourselves out of bed, and go to work. We cannot as moms say, "I just do not feel like being a mom today." We are always a mom, 24-7. By acknowledging that your child is tired or has a lot of homework and emphasizing the commitment and the need to fulfill it, you are teaching your child a valuable life lesson. Children need to recognize that their participation and effort are crucial to the team or the group's success.

When my son was playing lacrosse in high school, which required a daily commitment to practice, he was also taking many advanced classes that required a lot of homework each day. I helped him work out a schedule to fit it all in. Matthew would come home, do as much homework as he could, take a break, go to his practice or game, come back home, eat dinner, and then finish any remaining homework. If he knew what his practice and game schedules were for that week, and he knew what tests or projects were coming up that week, rather than devoting a big chunk of time the night before the test or project, he would divide his studying time or his time working on the project across multiple days. This allowed him to have time for games, practices, and schoolwork each day and to put forth his best effort on them all.

Someday, your children will likely work in an environment that requires collaboration and teamwork. You are giving them opportunities to learn these skills while growing up by encouraging them to participate in extracurricular activities. By being a part of a team, club, or group, your children will learn to put forth their best efforts to work toward a common goal.

Set the Right Priorities

If your children are busy with family responsibilities, schoolwork, and extracurricular activities, but you also want them to spend time with their family, you have to help them set the right priorities. They must be able to determine what is the most important to get accomplished that day, that week, or that month. Technology has a time and place in their lives but not at the expense of some of these other things.

It may be that when they look at their schedule for the day and see all the things that need to be done, they will see that there is not time to turn on the television or play video games. That is okay because it is more important for them to be involved in activities such as focusing on their schoolwork, fulfilling family responsibilities, and spending time with their family. With the invention of digital video recording (DVR), if there is something important that they need to see on television, then they can record it and set aside time on the weekend for viewing.

When my children were growing up, we had the rule of two when it came to extracurricular activities. That was because I did not want them taking on too many activities that would negatively impact their schoolwork or time with family. Also, since I was the chauffeur to all of my children's activities, I knew there was a limit to what I could do. My husband was traveling, so I did not usually have that extra parent to help out. My rule of two meant that each child was allowed to be in two extracurricular activities, maybe scouting and piano lessons or a sports team and a church group. Whatever was going to be a frequent and scheduled activity, each child was allowed to choose two of those.

Two multiplied by three children meant six extracurricular activities going on simultaneously. That was difficult to manage, but it was doable. If you need to, set a limit on what extracurricular activities your children can be involved in. If your children join a club at school that meets within school hours and does not require time outside of school, then you might not require that to be factored into the allotted number of extracurricular activities.

Make adjustments as necessary while still getting things done. It is okay to be flexible in your prearranged schedule, moving things around when necessary. Maybe your set schedule for doing homework a certain day needs to be adjusted because your child has a game or practice right in the middle of that allotted time. You are still teaching your child time management and that sometimes she has to be flexible and make adjustments, making sure that by the end of the day, the priorities are met and responsibilities are completed.

Schoolwork

I always think of school as our children's first job. They go to school just like they will go to work as adults. What your children do at school is their job, and they should be responsible about attending and completing any schoolwork to the best of their abilities.

You will likely encounter moments when your children come home with homework and are frustrated or tired, and you will want to step in and help them more than you should. Try to avoid doing that because it is not best for your child. It is okay to give them some support and offer suggestions that might help them, but taking over is not a good idea. The work should be theirs because that is in their best interest.

Set expectations for what they can accomplish and then support them. They might have a long-term project, writing a paper or studying for a test; help them figure out how they will divide up their time to meet the deadline and get it done. It is okay to give your advice and support them in that way because they are still the ones doing the work.

Helping your children study is always acceptable because they will still be the ones taking the test on their own; you will have just helped them prepare. One of my children was much more independent at studying, and the others liked me to quiz them with note cards they had made. This is an example of an acceptable way to help. My children had put the study tool in place; they just wanted my help in learning the information.

When your children are stuck on something or struggling, it is fine to help them figure it out. Your child might be struggling with a math problem or may not understand what a question is asking; it is acceptable to help your child determine how to work the problem or how to interpret the question. You are still letting your child do the work; you are just helping him think through the how.

Another way to support your children with schoolwork is to help them stay on track. This prevents them from ending up with too much to do at the last minute before a deadline, which will only work against them. You might notice your child is taking too many breaks or procrastinating, so you might encourage them by saying, "It would be better to just stick it out and get it done instead of procrastinating. You will be happier that you are finished."

Provide support and encouragement to help your children get their schoolwork completed, but do not rescue them. When you rescue your children, you send the message that you do not believe they can work through their own difficulties. Show your trust in their abilities to work through challenges and frustrations, and you will empower your children.

As an educator, I see the problems when parents rescue their children. My science teacher colleagues can easily recognize at science fair time which projects are the work of their students and which ones were completely done by the parents. If you recognize that you tend to step in to rescue your children, step away and put the focus back on them doing the work. In the end, they will feel empowered and will be much better off for it.

Your children must be responsible for their homework. That is part of their job as students. If they forget to do their homework and you notice their grades suffering for it, think about some things that you can do to help them remember their role and responsibility to complete their homework.

A dear friend knew this very well, and when her son Adam was in elementary school with my daughter, he began forgetting to bring the books home each day that he needed for homework. His mother told him, very clearly, that if he forgot his homework again, he was going to carry home every book in his desk for an entire week. That way, they could be sure he had everything he needed to do his homework successfully.

Despite the warning, Adam forgot his homework. My friend did exactly as promised and followed through with that discipline. She talked to Adam's teacher and told her that Adam would be bringing home every book in his desk for one week because he had been forgetting his homework, and she wanted to help him remember its importance. After a week of lugging home every book in his desk and then lugging them back the next morning, Adam learned the importance of having an organizational tool in place to help him remember his homework.

Our children are the future of the world. Teach them responsibility and help them grow into responsible adults. They must become adults who understand their role in the world—that they are responsible for doing their part in society, in the world, and in their own families.

When I was teaching in the South several years ago, I assigned a project to my students. I communicated the specific requirements for the project and included a rubric so that the students knew what points would be awarded for each requirement and how those points could be earned. I had a student who lost several points in one certain area on the rubric because she neglected to follow through on that required element.

When the student got her grade, it was much lower than her mother had expected. Her mother came marching into my classroom after school, very upset that her daughter had lost points on the project. The mom wanted to put the blame on me, telling me that I had been too harsh in grading her daughter. After listening to her mother direct the blame at me for a few minutes, the student said, "Mom, Mrs. Bartow told me what I needed to do. I knew what I needed to do. I am the one who chose not to do it."

In that moment, I was so impressed with that young lady. Here was a seventh-grade student recognizing that it was unfair for her mom to put the blame on me, and so she stepped up and claimed responsibility. Even though the mom was angry at me, I recognized that she had obviously done something right in raising her daughter. Even when her mom was trying to rescue her, that child stepped up and took responsibility. When her daughter spoke up, her mom accepted the grade, knowing she had overstepped her bounds. I commended the student on taking responsibility and silently hoped that her mom recognized *that* as much more important than the grade.

Consequences Are Heftier Later

When teaching your children responsibility, think about the ultimate goal because it is better for them to learn lessons about responsibility now than to learn them later. Even though it is not always easy to teach your child responsibility, especially when your child is in tears because she has to do a family chore instead of playing outside with her friends, you must stand firm and do what you know is right for her.

When Mary Kate was in high school, we moved to a new state for her sophomore year, and I wanted her to get involved so that she could adjust more quickly. Since I was a teacher in the same community, I would hear about her classmates having parties on the weekends, and I was concerned that she was choosing to stay at home rather than go. After watching her pass on several parties in as many weeks, I asked her, "Why don't you go to any of the parties your classmates are having? You know, Amy is having a party this weekend." I continued encouraging her, thinking I was doing the right thing. I wanted her to get out and meet new people and overcome the shyness I thought she was experiencing because she was new to the school.

Finally, one day she said to me, "I am not going to those parties because there is alcohol at those parties, everyone is drinking, and I do not want to feel the peer pressure."

I was so proud of her for being responsible. She knew that by going to the parties, she could meet people and make friends, but she did not want to put herself in a situation where there was underage drinking. We had been raising her to be responsible, and when faced with a difficult decision, she had put that teaching into practice and made the responsible decision not to attend. Difficulty is okay. Your children are going to be challenged and put in difficult situations. That is part of teaching them to be responsible.

For the first two years of Matthew's high school career, Meghan was his transportation to and from school each day. When Meghan graduated, Matthew was not quite old enough to drive, and my job did not allow me to be at the bus stop right when he got off the bus. Since he was attending private school, we were lucky to have a bus, but the bus dropped off at a local shopping center a few miles from our house.

In those few months, I had to be clear that I could not get there in time to pick him up when the bus dropped him off, so he had two choices. He could sit at a coffee shop in the shopping center and wait for me, or he could walk the few miles home. Most of those afternoons, he chose to walk home. Yes, those extra few miles were a difficulty for him, especially after a long day at school and while lugging a heavy backpack, but he needed to get himself home. That was the price he decided to pay rather than wait the extended time required for me to pick him up.

When our children were teenagers, my husband and I set a curfew because we did not feel teenagers should be out at all hours. As they also began driving, we wanted to instill responsibility by setting a time that they had to be home. On school nights, we were stricter on that time because they had homework and family responsibilities and needed to get to bed at a decent time. Social activities during the week were limited as well. On the weekends, social activities were encouraged because we wanted our children to have time to spend with their friends.

The curfews we set were age specific and based on their maturity level and concerns about what they might be exposed to after certain hours. Our children knew that if they broke their curfews, there would be consequences. If you set a curfew for your children, expect your children to abide by it. Remember—a rule that is not enforced is no longer a rule.

When my son first got his driver's license, he was so excited, as any teenager would be. The first Friday night after getting his license, Matthew had plans to meet some friends at his high school's football game and then head home. We reminded him what time he needed to be home as he headed out that night. About fifteen minutes before his curfew, he called and said he was stuck in traffic and would be a bit later. When Matthew got home, my husband and I were waiting. Matthew explained that he had gone to a restaurant after the game and had lost track of time. We reminded him quite firmly, "You had a curfew in place. It is your responsibility, no matter what is going on, to get home on time. You must make allowances for traffic and other unforeseen delays. This is your one mess-up. If you miss curfew again, you will not be driving for two weeks."

About a week later, my husband was out of town. Matthew was headed out with friends, and I reminded him about his curfew. As the curfew approached later that night, I sat there watching the clock because I knew that if he came in late, he would not be going anywhere for two weeks. I looked at the clock, sighed out loud, and said under my breath, "He is going to miss his curfew again."

My daughter said, "Mom, look at the clock on your computer, which is the satellite time. He actually has two minutes."

She was right. One minute later, the garage door opened, and my son walked in the door exactly on the dot of his curfew. His eyes were so big, and he said, "I made it, Mom. I got home by my curfew."

We had instilled in our son the importance of being responsible and adhering to his curfew. We also made clear what the consequences would be if he didn't. We did the same with all of our children so that they were very aware that if they missed their curfew, there would be a consequence for it.

Volunteer

Children need to learn to help others and be responsible for the world that they live in. One of the easiest ways to help your children learn to serve others and be in service to their world is to encourage them to volunteer their time. They can volunteer their talent as well, singing in the church choir, serving at the altar at church, being a peer tutor, volunteering at a hospital or nursing home, or otherwise giving of themselves and helping the less fortunate. They can help at a soup kitchen or a food bank. When they are volunteering their time and talents, they are learning to give of themselves.

When Meghan was in middle school, she started teaching every summer at Vacation Bible School. She loved children, and she wanted to share her faith, so teaching at her church during the summer was a perfect fit. She developed lesson plans, she got up early on summer mornings, she arrived on time each day, and she cared for and guided young children through learning about their faith. By giving up a week of her summer to help kids, she learned to be responsible. She was learning, too, how to give of herself and her talents to help others.

For the good of the world, children cannot be raised without compassion for others. Instill in your children that they have to be compassionate, helping humanity and those less fortunate. Part of that is teaching them to be responsible. Whether they volunteer weekly, monthly, or in the summer, that is up to you.

Help them carve out time in their lives to be of service and share their talents with others. Encourage them to do so starting at a young age so that the practice will continue throughout their lives. If they learn at a young age, *I need to volunteer, I need to help others, and I need to give time without getting paid for it because it is the right thing to do,* then those ideals will carry over into their adult lives and make them compassionate adults.

When your children are giving their time to help others, they are learning responsibility and building their character. Compassionate adults will care for others and the world around them. Teach your children to be good people with strong morals and compassion for others.

Do Not Make Excuses; Hold Them Accountable

Hold your children accountable so that they learn responsibility. If they are doing poorly in school, they must be held accountable. Ask them what they need to do differently to improve, and avoid blaming the teacher. Focus on your child, the student, and what he is or is not doing to get himself in this predicament, and then find out what changes he can make to do better in school.

Your children are the ones in school, not you. They are listening to the teacher every day. They hear her instructions, her timetables for when things are due, and the importance of different assignments and how to complete them. You are not in the classroom hearing those things, and it is unfair to assume you know how your child behaves or performs at school. It is unfair to think that it is the teacher's fault. As your children grow up and enter the work world, if they do something poorly and their boss comes down on them, it will not be the boss's fault.

Children must learn from an early age that they will be held accountable and that they must fulfill their responsibilities. They cannot blame others when things don't go well or when they fail at something. If your child is struggling in school, help her work through whatever that struggle is. Help her make the changes she needs to do better. In so doing, you are teaching her that she is accountable for her actions and will be responsible for making amends and changing her actions when necessary.

When your children are younger especially, you might offer ideas of things they can do or help them brainstorm solutions. Maybe they are not studying enough, not spending adequate time on homework, or not following the teacher's instructions. You might say to them, "You need to go talk to your teacher about this. Ask her what you need to do to bring up your grade." It is the child's responsibility to follow through on the suggestion.

It is empowering for your children to learn to face the music, even if it might be uncomfortable for them. They might get a stern lecture from their teacher for misbehaving in class. They might get a zero because they did not do their homework, or they might get a poor grade on a test because they did not study appropriately. When those grades come and you are talking to them about what they need to do differently or about the improvements they can make on their own, they will make those changes because they will not want to face those consequences again.

If my children ever came home with stories about their teachers, going on and on about how mean a teacher was or saying something like, "Mrs. Smith yelled at me today, and I didn't even do anything," I would respond, "So if I call Mrs. Smith, is she going to tell me the same thing?"

Usually that was enough to help them temper their story and get a bit closer to the truth about what had actually happened. There are always two sides to every story. Children are very good at embellishing. Help them think about what really happened. You might ask, "Do you think there was a reason that Mrs. Smith responded in that way?"

As they get older, teach your children to advocate for themselves and accept the decisions that result. When they get to the upper elementary grades and especially middle school, they should be learning to do this. This can even start younger on a smaller scale. If your child is struggling in school, then teach her to talk to the teacher and ask what she can do. If your child comes home and tells you that his teacher got upset at him for something, ask him to talk to his teacher. If your child feels that a teacher was unfair, encourage her to go talk to the teacher about it. By following through with your suggestions, your children are learning to advocate for themselves, and you can still be there to help them if they need to talk it through with you.

While teaching middle-school students, nothing makes me happier than for them to take the initiative and come to me themselves when they have a question or need help. If students have a question about a grade they received, or they don't understand something, or they need clarification on what they need to do to improve, they will come to me and say, "Mrs.

Bartow, I just don't understand how to do this project" or "I don't understand what I need to do differently on my rough draft." That is much more powerful than the parent calling and saying, "My child does not understand how to do this essay."

The parent is not in the classroom with me. The parent does not hear my instructions, but the student does. If I explain the instructions directly to the student because he asked, he will understand much more quickly because he was there for all of the background instruction in the classroom. The student will understand as I now explain the specifics that will help him get past the hurdle that has him stuck. A parent will not understand because the parent was not there.

Whenever you can, encourage your children to advocate for themselves with their teachers. For example, "Mrs. Jones, will you look at this test? You counted me off a few points on my answer to question 10. Will you look at my answer again and explain what I was missing so I don't make the same mistake next time? Or can I do anything to help me get some of those points back?"

Once the teacher has made her decision and communicated that to your child, your child has to accept that decision. The teacher might say, "I reviewed your answer, and it is incorrect because you did not answer the question asked. It would be unfair to give you points back when other students do not have that opportunity, but I would encourage you to do the extra credit I offered last week."

Part of teaching your children to advocate for themselves is teaching them that they will not always get the answer they want, but they can be proud of taking responsibility and talking to their teacher. At other times, the decision will be in their favor. Either way, they have to learn to accept that decision. That is the way life is; decisions do not always go in your favor. If your children have advocated for themselves, they have already done an important thing. Praise them for that.

When parents get too involved or advocate on behalf of their children, oftentimes the children do not follow through because they do not have any vested interest. As a teacher, I have received phone calls from parents asking if there is any extra credit their child can do because their child did poorly on a test. I have then outlined for the parents the extra credit opportunities. In those instances, more often than not, the child does not ever complete the extra credit offered. Why? It was the parent who wanted the child to do that extra credit. It was the mom calling me instead of encouraging the child to advocate for himself. However, if the parent says to the child, "If you want to try to bring up your grade, contact Mrs. Bartow and ask her if there is any extra credit you can do," the child is more likely to follow through.

If the child wants to do extra credit and asks for it, she has that vested interest and is more likely to complete it. She has advocated for herself, she appreciates firsthand the opportunity that the teacher has extended to her, and she does not want to let the teacher down.

When my son was in tenth grade, I met with his English teacher at a parent–teacher conference. The teacher told me how much he respected my son. He said, "I had a conversation with Matthew about his essay." He explained that my son had e-mailed him asking about his essay in a disrespectful way. The teacher replied to my son, telling him that the way he was asking was not appropriate. Matthew responded, "I should know better than to respond in a disrespectful way to my teacher since my mom is a teacher too. I am so sorry. If there is something I can do to raise my grade, I would really appreciate the opportunity."

I did not know anything about this until I heard it from the teacher at that parent–teacher conference. My son had never mentioned it to me. As the teacher told me this and told me how impressed he was with my son's handling of the situation, I was so proud. Had my son done something wrong? Yes! He had replied to the teacher disrespectfully. However, when the teacher brought it to his attention, my son had apologized, responded in an appropriate way, and advocated for himself. He did not come to me and say, "Mom, Mr. Jones told me I was being disrespectful." He did not ask me to get involved. He recognized that he had made a mistake and responded appropriately. That helped the teacher see Matthew in a new light and respect him even more, which is what I had always hoped when teaching my children to advocate for themselves.

My oldest daughter was a rule follower throughout her years in school and did not get into trouble at school. However, when Meghan was in eleventh grade, she got her first detention for wearing her uniform skirt too short. School policy required that the skirts be worn at least at a certain length, but she and her friends wanted to wear the skirts shorter. Each day after getting to school, the girls would roll up their waistbands to make their skirts shorter. Meghan got detention for that infraction, and she was not happy about it. When she got home, she said, "I got a detention because I wore my skirt too short. I have to serve detention tomorrow, which isn't fair since every girl rolls her skirt."

My response was to remind her that she knew the rule about the required length of the skirt, and she had chosen to roll it up anyway. The consequence was that she would have to serve the detention. It didn't matter that other girls were doing it. Her choice, her consequence.

Your children will make bad decisions, but if they are held accountable and they face up to the consequences, they will learn from their mistakes. When my youngest daughter was in high school, I noticed that homework was being missed too frequently. I had to step in and say, "If you miss your homework one more time, you will lose social privileges after school for two weeks." My daughter knew that I would be checking her online grade book daily to make sure homework was getting done. I encouraged her to spend adequate time each day on her homework so she would be prepared at school. In no time, my daughter was back on track and getting her homework completed.

Your children must be held accountable so they learn that there are consequences to their behavior. Do not make excuses for them, and do not rescue them. Your children are the future of the world; they are responsible for living their lives, fulfilling their responsibilities, and fulfilling their commitments and obligations. When you raise responsible children, everyone will benefit from that. Your children will be the future leaders of the world. It takes only one glance at the headlines to see what happens when people have not learned to take responsibility for their actions. When a person's go-to response is to make excuses or blame someone else, that person has not learned responsibility.

Give your children the gift of responsibility so they know it is not okay to blame others for something they have done wrong. It is not okay to ignore problems. It is more important, even when it is uncomfortable and difficult, to teach your children to be responsible and own their actions.

Chapter Six
The Gift of Goals and Work Ethic

*No matter how you feel, get up, dress
up, show up, and never give up.*
—Unknown

Make It Part of the Conversation and Start Early

When Matthew was just three years old, he became so enamored with the garbage collectors. He loved watching the garbage men ride on the back of the garbage truck, hop off, throw the trash in the truck, and jump back on the truck. He thought that was the most wonderful job. He would tell me that when he grew up, he wanted to be a garbage man. I would say to him, "That is absolutely fine if that is what you choose to do, as long as you have a college degree."

In our family, a college degree was a goal for all of our children; it was an expectation from us as parents. From the earliest moments, that conversation about college after high school was present. "When you graduate from high school, you will go on to college and get to study what you want to do for your career."

When Meghan graduated from high school and some of her classmates were stopping there and not continuing on to college, she actually said, "Mom! I had forgotten that ending your education after high school was a possibility!" It was so ingrained in our children from the earliest age that they were going to college that she did not even remember that college was optional.

Whatever the goal is for your children, whatever you want them to accomplish, start that conversation early. We wanted a college education for our children, so all through their lives, we talked about it. Even though the focus of those conversations was getting a bachelor's degree, none of our children stopped there. They wanted to gain more knowledge and be prepared for their chosen professions, and that required additional education in the form of advanced degrees, which they all earned.

Long-Term and Short-Term Goals

Your children must have goals. Whether they are long-term or short-term, both are needed. The long-term goals might take months or years to accomplish. Short-term goals might be accomplished in a few days or weeks. Having goals gives your children a direction, a path to take. If they set goals for themselves, they will be working toward something. They will have purpose in their lives because they will have a focus on what they want to achieve. Encourage your children to set goals and put in the work that will help them be successful because, whatever the goal, work will be required.

Your children's long-term goals might include earning a specific degree, graduating from high school, getting into a good college, or getting a specific job. Whatever their goals are, they will be working toward them for a number of years. Encourage your children and support them in working to achieve their long-term goals.

Short-term goals give your children something to work toward day to day, and they will see the rewards of their efforts more quickly. A short-term goal might be to earn a spot on a sports team in school, get elected to a leadership position in a club, or finish an important project and earn a good grade. Support your children by helping them figure out how much extra practice they need to put in before tryouts, by reviewing their campaign speech with them, and by helping them prioritize getting the project done. If your child wants to make all As by the end of the semester, you could ask her how much extra study time she thinks she needs to put in to achieve that.

Both short-term goals and long-term goals provide opportunities for your children to set their sights on something, focus their energy, and put in the effort to achieve the goal. Children who set goals will learn the value of effort. Even if they don't reach a goal, they can take comfort in knowing they did everything they could to achieve it and feel pride in that.

Even When Children Are Not Successful, Learning Is the Valuable Lesson

Maybe your child has a short-term goal of making the basketball team. You can help him put a plan in place. He determines the need to practice a specified amount of time every day, do extra drills, and practice with his dad on weekends. Whatever he thinks is needed to reach that goal, he will take steps to make that happen.

Your child might want to make the soccer team or cheerleading squad, or she might want a part in the school play. Even if after all of the time and effort, she does not make the team or squad or does not get that part in the play, she will benefit because she set that goal, focused on something that she wanted, and put in the required effort to achieve it. She can still be proud of the work that she put in.

Support your children in creating a plan to achieve goals and follow through with the plan. Help your children understand the value of the work they put in. You might say, "Even though you did not achieve something you wanted, you still did something very valuable for yourself. Even though you put in that extra time with the drills and extra practice for the basketball team and did not make it, you still learned some great skills. You are now a better basketball player than you were."

In situations such as these, encourage your child to keep practicing and try out again next time. If it was the cheerleading squad, encourage your child to keep learning the cheers and try out again next year. If your child did not get the part in the play, remind her that there will be another play. Stress what valuable skills your child learned while putting in the extra time.

Children will succeed in life when they first recognize that in working to achieve their goals, sometimes they will fall short. That does not mean that the goal was not worth having. Your children will still have moved toward something and exercised determination and diligence in the effort and energy they put into reaching the goal. Children will learn that sometimes, they need to rework or revise their goals.

Life is about learning that even when you work hard to achieve something, you do not always get what you want. You will not always find success at everything you try, but there can be learning in failure too. When your children work very hard for something and do not get it, they learn that things will still be okay. They learn to think about failure in new ways: *I really wanted to make the team, and I really worked hard to get there, but I am still okay even though I did not make the team. Mom still loves me, and now I am going to change things up and work harder and try again.*

The value comes in the message your children learn when they set and work toward goals, even if they don't quite achieve them. The valuable message for your children is that the importance is in trying their best. If they give it their all, work hard, and miss the goal, they can still be proud of what they accomplished, even if they did not make the team or get the part in the play. Every time your child sets a goal and works toward reaching that goal, he or she is growing as a person.

Getting and Keeping a Job

Along with goals, your children must have a strong work ethic, which is such a necessity throughout life, starting with their first job, which is school. Think of them getting up every day and going to school just as they will get up every day and go to work when they get older. Make sure that they are putting in the effort, maintaining a good work ethic, and striving to do their best in school.

Think about what your children are capable of, and set expectations for their grades. If your expectation is no less than a B on their report card because you know they are capable of that, communicate that expectation and support them in achieving that. If you expect them to behave and be respectful, communicate that as well.

You know your children and where their struggles are. If they have difficulties in learning, if school is problematic for them, then you know about that. Set goals for them that are challenging but achievable. Strong work ethic will come from working toward goals.

In my family, zeros for homework were not acceptable. I would say to my children, "Homework is the easy part of your grade. All you have to do is complete it and turn it in." I explained that homework was the practice that would help them do better on their tests or the assignments that would count for more. Because zeros for homework were not acceptable, their work ethic was being strengthened; they knew that they did not have the option of not doing an assignment. My children knew that if they chose not to do an assignment, there would be consequences.

Homework was part of my children's job at school, and they had to do their job. I was preparing them for when they became adults because adults must be able to get and keep a job. Adults also must complete all parts of their jobs, even the parts they don't like very much, like children and homework.

Many people I have known personally are able to get jobs, but when it comes to keeping the jobs, they have difficulty. A couple of weeks after being hired, they are looking for work again, and many times, it is because they were let go for excessive tardiness, not doing the required tasks, calling in sick too much, and the list goes on. Ensure that your children will be adults who can keep a job. They have to be able to support their families and provide for themselves. They need to put food on the table, and the way they do that is by keeping a job.

If you have worked, you have probably worked with someone who had a poor work ethic and have felt the exasperation that comes along with that. These are the workers who are consistently late to work or who do not care about getting the job done right. That means someone else has to pick up the slack, and that might just be you, especially if you work together on a team. Poor work ethic can be seen in workers who do not feel they have to follow the company rules and policies or who frequently try to get out of tasks. To them, the job is just something for which they show up and put in their time; they are not contributing to the organization or doing their best. They are taking away from others when they do not pull their weight and instead leave someone else to make up for their inadequacies.

After my daughter Meghan had decided to go to grad school, she was trying to figure out ways to support herself while in school; she got a job at a restaurant, which was a first for her. She started out as a hostess and realized that she could not make as much money in that position as she could as a server. Since she had learned to advocate for herself as a child, she went to her boss and said, "I need to make more money. Is there any way that I could be considered for a server position?" At that point, Meghan had been working at the restaurant for a couple of months, and her boss had seen her strong work ethic. Her boss agreed to promote her to server.

A few months into waitressing, my daughter was struggling. Waitressing was more difficult than she had anticipated. Each time her boss called her in to talk over something that she was doing wrong, it negatively affected her. She lost her confidence and began thinking she just couldn't do it. Before long, this became a self-fulfilling prophecy, and after several discussions with her boss, my daughter felt certain that she would be let go from her position if she made one more mistake.

It was coming up on Christmas break, and Meghan decided to take the rest of the week off and head home. She thought her days were numbered at this job. She came home with that frustration and told me about how much she was struggling as a waitress, explaining that she did not think she could be a good server.

I talked her through her options. By talking about it, she realized that there were not many options in her small college town that would give her the flexibility she needed to attend school and also would pay as well as her current waitressing job. She recognized that she had to make this work.

Meghan and I talked about what she thought she could do to keep her job and do well in the position. She decided to talk to her boss and explain her commitment and desire to work hard so that she could become a good waitress. When she returned to her job after Christmas break, she walked into her boss's office and said, "I know I have been struggling in this position, but I am committed to doing a good job and doing whatever it takes to be a good server."

The boss knew Meghan had a good work ethic; she had seen it in action for months when Meghan worked as a hostess for the restaurant. Meghan's boss appreciated her commitment and decided to give her the chance to prove she could do it. The boss offered to retrain her and then wipe the slate clean and allow Meghan to start fresh. At that point, my daughter knew she had to make this work. She did what she needed to do and became very successful in that job.

A few months later, Meghan was employee of the month. Within a year, she was a trainer herself, and not long after that, she was promoted to shift lead. My daughter proved to herself that she could do anything when she set her mind to it.

Instill a strong work ethic in your children so that they are able to put forth the effort that will be required to do the best job they can at every job they have in life. Children should not be raised to think they are "above" doing menial tasks. Nothing should be beneath them because even though they might think that one day they will be doctors, lawyers, business owners, or government leaders, they will gain invaluable experience and appreciation from doing some of those menial jobs. Children should learn there is pride in any job if they are giving it their best.

Examples of Not Having These Consequences

When I was working at a school in the Midwest, there was a teacher on staff who had earned the reputation of not pulling his weight. Everybody was aware that he would shirk responsibility as often as he could. When it was time for a group project, he was going to ask others to do his part for him. The sad thing was that people would do it for him. What he learned was that if he shirked his responsibility and asked others to do his part, they would do it for him. He never had a consequence for not doing the work because someone would always rescue him.

Even in the adult world, you see people who were not raised to have goals or a strong work ethic. I have a friend who has a hard time following authority. She never learned growing up that you must listen to authority, but part of a good work ethic is being able to take direction from your boss and follow through with that. Not being able to follow authority has certainly hindered her in her professional growth.

I have another friend who has a hard time keeping a job. Again, that strong work ethic has never been there. If the job is not perfect, he wants to quit the job. The problem is that no job is perfect. Even our roles as moms are not perfect. If your children think that everything is going to be fun, glorious, and wonderful every day in every goal or job that they have, then they have been set up for failure because that is not the real world. Your children must have a strong work ethic even when the task at hand is not one that they particularly enjoy.

You have likely heard various workplace excuses: "If they are going to make that change, then I am not going to do it" or "If they are going to make that a new responsibility for my job and not pay me extra, then I will refuse to do it." These are the excuses of people who do not have a strong work ethic instilled in them, the work ethic that tells them that if a task or responsibility is part of their job, then it is necessary, and they need to follow through on it.

Every time somebody in an organization fails to pull his weight, it is a drain on everybody. The negativity and the failure to fulfill the responsibility impact everyone, and someone else is left to clean up the mess. Raise your children to fulfill their responsibilities and make positive contributions in their jobs. Teach them to set goals, and instill in them that strong work ethic.

Delayed Gratification and Appreciation

To help your children be successful on the job, raise them to recognize that work will not always have an instant reward. They might work for a long time before they see a reward, or more often than not, there will not be any reward at all other than that intrinsic motivation and pride that comes from a job well done. Raise your children to work hard because the work they do has value, not because they will get a reward for it.

From school to work, your children must wait to get rewarded, and very often, they will not get rewarded at all. You can teach them to appreciate the efforts that they put into a job or project. Teach them to think, *If I have done my very best, put in my best effort to do the job, then that is something to be proud of and appreciate about myself.*

At the same time, your children should learn to appreciate everyone's efforts. If your child is working on a group project and everyone is doing their part, your child must appreciate the work that is done by everyone else. Even if it is not done the exact way that she would have done it, she must appreciate that others are contributing something valuable.

When your children learn to wait to be rewarded or that they can work without being rewarded, a strong work ethic is alive in them. When your children learn to appreciate the efforts of others and work with others to get the job done, that further builds on the foundation of that work ethic. When they value their own best efforts, they have learned that a strong work ethic is a reward in itself.

Natural Progression

When your children are old enough, encourage them to get a job so they can learn valuable skills and get a taste of what it will be like in the real world. If they are given the gift of responsibility, then it is a natural progression to have goals and a strong work ethic. These traits go hand in hand with one another. It is healthy for your children to have tough jobs. It is healthy for them to work hard at something, even menial tasks. This will help them to see the value in education, responsibility, and their own efforts.

Tough jobs are more than acceptable; they are character-building. When my children were old enough to take on jobs, they had jobs in factories, restaurants, and retail. Even as they were studying in college, they had these jobs. They were working toward advanced degrees and holding down some of these jobs. They did not think these jobs were beneath them. Instead, they thought that these jobs would be a great way to earn money and learn skills, even if they were not skills needed for their chosen careers.

Working hard and having a strong work ethic are lifelong characteristics needed by everyone. Your children need to learn that if they take on a job, they must do their best at that job and be a responsible employee. They will learn these skills on the job.

If you are worried about your teenagers taking on jobs that may impact their schoolwork, you might encourage them to get summer jobs. Even if your children work those tough jobs only in the summer or during school breaks, they will still learn something very valuable. They will learn what it takes to earn money and keep a job. They will begin to understand how much effort goes into every dollar that they earn and the skills required to keep a job. That will help them appreciate the value of a dollar, which will serve them well as adults.

If a child has a strong work ethic, that will translate to anything that the child undertakes in his life, whether your child is working through college or grad school or working to expand his career. That will be a gift that will keep on giving for his whole lifetime because everyone recognizes someone who has a good work ethic.

People with strong work ethics are the people whom the bosses of the world appreciate, give extra responsibility to, and promote up the corporate ladder. They will be the ones the boss goes to when he wants something done well. The employees with a strong work ethic are the ones who earn the promotions, the raises, and the recognition. Help your children learn a strong work ethic because they should always want to put their best foot forward and do their best work.

How I Was Raised

When I was growing up, we were expected to get good grades. That was just a given. Our parents expected nothing less. When we were old enough, we were expected to get a job. In my case, as soon as I was old enough, I started babysitting. When I got into high school, I worked retail. Even though jobs such as those in stores and restaurants require children to be sixteen years of age, there are jobs that your children can do in middle school such as mowing lawns, babysitting, dog sitting, and pet walking.

When I was hired for my first job, I did not even have a car to get myself to that job. But I needed the money, so I was not going to let transportation stop me. I figured out a way, and usually that meant walking to work, which was several miles away. If I had to be at work at a certain time, I had to factor in how long it would take to walk there. Other times, I was able to coordinate rides to or from work with other people who worked at the store with me and who lived near me. I needed to keep that job, so I was willing to do whatever it took to keep it.

When I was growing up, there was no extra money to buy me a car. If I wanted a car, I would have to pay for it myself, which is where the job came in. I knew in the beginning that it would be hard because I could not get myself to that job unless I walked to it. My whole goal was to earn money so that I could buy a car.

When I had finally saved enough money to buy my own car and was making enough money to make the monthly payments, I made a trip to the car dealership to pick out a car. I found a car I liked, looked at all the features on the car and the price for each, and then said to the salesman, "Well, how much cheaper will it be if I get the car without automatic transmission?"

I did not even know how to drive a stick shift, but I knew I was going to have to make some adjustments if I was going to afford that car. The salesman told me the price of the car without automatic transmission, and it was still more than I could afford. I thought for a minute and then said, "How much would the car cost without air-conditioning?"

The salesman looked at me as if I had lost my mind; this was Louisiana after all. He soon realized I was serious, and he gave me the price. Finally, a price I could afford! So I bought a car that had no air-conditioning and no automatic transmission. Because I did not know how to drive a stick shift, I could not even drive my car off the lot. No one in my family knew how to drive a stick shift either, so the salesman drove the car home for me. My boyfriend then took me into a parking lot and spent days teaching me how to drive my car with manual transmission.

I had learned the gift of having goals and a strong work ethic from my parents. Even though it was difficult, I had walked to work for months until I had earned enough to buy a car without air-conditioning and without automatic transmission. I needed the car for the job, and I needed the job for the car.

Not Entitled; Must Work for It

Nothing destroys a child's work ethic faster than a sense of entitlement. Your children should not feel entitled to anything. If they want something in life, they must work for it. As moms, you have the power to instill this in your children.

When my husband was growing up, he worked in his family business. With five children in the family, money was tight, so when he was a teenager, he saved enough money to buy his own car. After high school, he was struggling with how he would afford college tuition. He sat out of college for a while and learned the skill of welding. After about eighteen months, he decided he wanted to go to college. By that time, he was making some money and saving some money, so he had enough to go to college.

Raise your children with the understanding that they are not entitled to anything from society or from their parents. You can still provide extras that you can afford, but these things should feel like gifts to your children, not things to which they are entitled. We were blessed to be able to do more for our kids than had been done for us as children, but we still expected our children to work and pull their weight within the family. We did not raise them to feel entitled to anything.

Give your children the gift of goals and a strong work ethic. No one in the world is entitled to anything. Your children are not entitled to a new car, good grades, an expensive pair of shoes, or a good job. Your children must work for these things in one way or another. If your children learn this, your children and our world will be better for it.

Chapter Seven
The Gift of a United Front

The best security blanket a child can have
is parents who respect each other.
—Jane Blaustone

Children Recognize a Chink in the Armor

A powerful gift that you give your children is the gift of a united front, which means that you and your coparent stand united in decisions in front of your children. Children recognize when there is a chink in the armor. They recognize when there is a weakness that they can use to their advantage, and they will.

The armor that you and your coparent have is the united front that you present to your children; it prevents your children from being able to manipulate you. Children should not learn to be manipulators; they should not get anything in life because they manipulated somebody to get it. Manipulation is a negative trait, so take steps to ensure that your children do not learn to use it.

When you and your coparent present a united front, your children will not be able to use one parent against the other. Whoever is helping to raise your children must be on the same page as you. Whatever answers the children get from one of you, they should know they will get the same answers from the other if they ask.

Coparents Will Not Always Agree

Coparents will not always agree on every decision that they make when it comes to their children; two different individuals will not always have the same ideas. However, you must come together on how you will address issues with your children. You must agree to address topics in a way that presents a united front.

Presenting a united front requires that even though you may disagree on issues, you will come together and put a plan in place for how to address those topics. Some topics will be areas of disagreement from the beginning when you are discussing how to raise your children. These topics might relate to religion, how you will discipline, or influences you will or will not allow. On the other hand, you will have some larger issues about which you are both already on the same page. You can already nail down those specific topics. Understand that you will not have a blueprint for every single issue or topic that will come along. That would be unrealistic. Your children are individual and unique and will change as they grow, so new issues will arise all the time.

If you have come together on the larger issues, you will at least have a working foundation. That is what is important. Think about the larger issues—religion, discipline, financial issues, and education. Have a working foundation for those things, and then you can address other issues as they come along. As mentioned earlier, my husband and I had different views on discipline, and we made the effort to come together on the issue of spanking.

Keep in mind that you and your coparent are in this together, and you are not enemies. You are not on opposite sides. You may disagree on an issue, but you are on the same side because you both want what is best for your children. You must work together and work through issues for the good of your children because a united front is crucial.

Going with the One Who Feels More Strongly

One way to ensure that you present a united front when there are issues you disagree on is to go with which one of you feels more strongly about it. As your children are growing, there will be issues that you are not prepared for. When raising our children, my husband and I knew the direction we wanted to take with our children on the larger issues. Sometimes, however, especially as our children became teenagers, my husband and I struggled to find the correct response or solution; that exact right response would elude us. An issue might arise that I wanted to discuss with my husband, to weigh the pros and cons with him before responding to the children. Or there might be an issue on which we differed regarding what the correct response should be. Whenever we had those discussions where we were trying to come to a decision, we always had them out of earshot of our children.

When those issues arise that have you and your coparent disagreeing on how best to approach them, take steps to prevent your children from seeing you disagree. In front of your children, you must present a united front. Those discussions about how to proceed take place behind closed doors. Whether there is a struggle over how to respond, a need to weigh the pros and cons together, or a wish to bounce ideas off one another, do that behind closed doors.

Minor everyday decisions were easily addressed by either me or my husband. We had a strong foundation and knew how we wanted to raise our children and respond to issues. However, sometimes the topics, questions, or needs required a more thoughtful response. If my children asked me something that caught me off-guard, raising a significant issue that required time to ponder and determine the best response, I would say, "I want to talk this over with your dad before I respond. I want to have time to think about it. Your dad and I will talk about it, and we will let you know our decision."

After my husband and I had had a chance to talk about it and the decision was made, we would come back to the children, tell them that we had discussed the issue, and communicate our decision to them. Sometimes my husband and I were easily in agreement; other times, we felt differently and had our own individual reasons for our thinking. In those latter instances, we would voice our concerns and opinions to each other, and if we couldn't reach a mutual decision, we would go with the decision of the one of us who felt the strongest about the issue. We both loved our children and wanted what was best for them, so we trusted each other enough to do that. When we then told the children our decision, the children had no idea that we were on opposite sides of the issue. They just knew that we had talked about it and come to a decision and that they were expected to abide by the decision we had made.

Since children are not always known for their patience, you will likely have moments when your children will demand a response on the spot. After telling your child you want to talk with her dad and will then let her know, you might still hear, "But I want to know right now—can I go to the concert with Sasha on a school night? Can I go? She needs an answer now!"

When my children pushed me like that, I would tell them, "If I have to answer right now, the answer is going to be no. If I have a chance to think about it and talk it over with your dad, then the answer might be different." Whatever works for you as a response will be appropriate, but have a response ready.

If your children demand an answer on the spot and you are not comfortable answering in the moment because you want to think about it or discuss with the coparent, then tell them exactly that. Take that time when you need it so that you will respond with confidence rather than rushing a decision you will regret or that you know your coparent will not agree with. You certainly do not want the coparent to feel like you have done something behind his back when you have agreed to talk through big issues together.

Divided behind Closed Doors

When you are divided on an issue, the children do not need to know who stood where on what topic. They do not need to know that Mom did not want them to go on the campout and Dad felt it would be fine to go. They need to know only that you came to a united decision and that the decision is X.

Be aware that sometimes your children will figure it out anyway. They have been raised by you and your coparent, and they will recognize the differences between you. My children tended to recognize that I would be the stricter parent on most topics. As their mom, I was more aware of their personality traits and how they responded to different situations. I knew who their friends were, so I knew what some of the pressures might be. As an educator, I knew what was going on in the community, so I was aware of situations they could get themselves into that were not good. I tended to be the stricter parent because I was aware of all those things. My children knew that.

By the time they got into their teen years, they really had it figured out. If I said then that Dad and I were going to talk about an issue before deciding, they knew in their minds, *Mom will be pushing for a stricter response.* However, those discussions still took place out of earshot, and they still saw a united front. If one of our children said, "Dad would let me do this," I would respond, "Your dad and I made this decision together, and he is in support of the decision."

Even when the decision was mine alone, if a child ever said, "Dad would let me do it," I would respond, "Your dad will support the decision I made." My children saw that in action as well. It wasn't just words.

Make sure that you and your coparent back each other up in your decisions because your children will test you on this. If you have told them they can't do something, they may say, "Dad would let me do it." Your response has to be that you and your coparent are a team. If you have made a decision, your coparent will back you up. If it is a decision that you and your coparent want to discuss first, you will discuss the situation and let your children know the decision. Your children must know that you and your coparent will back each other up, whatever the decision is. Never make your coparent look bad in front of your children. That will be a detriment to your children and prevent them from seeing a united front.

As our son was a senior in high school and beginning to narrow down his college options, we were in the process of moving between states. Our son wanted to go to the university in the state where we were currently living. Many of his friends were headed there, and he wanted to go too. We knew that moving out of state would make tuition unattainable for us financially since we would have to pay the higher out-of-state rate. We did not give him the option of going to the university in the state that we were moving from.

One day, I was in the car running errands with my son. He was so angry and disappointed about not being able to attend the state university. He said to me, "If I talk to Dad about this, he will let me go."

I replied, "Your dad and I have already talked about this, and this is the decision that we made together. We wish you could attend the university, but we will not be able to afford the out-of-state tuition. We need for you to explore universities in the state we are moving to and other private universities where you will be eligible for a scholarship."

My husband and I had already had the conversation, and even though my son hoped he could get a different response from his dad, he soon realized that the decision was made and would not be changing.

When our children were old enough to date, I knew what pressures were out there, and I knew what the dangers could be. My husband was a bit more laid-back about it, so again, we had that discussion behind closed doors. We had to decide what the rules would be for our children when they reached dating age. Once we had come to an agreement, we presented those rules to our children with a united front.

When it came to deciding curfews, my husband and I again had differing opinions to start. My husband had grown up in a house where the girls had a curfew and the boys did not. Right away, I knew I did not want a double standard for our children, and I felt very strongly about that. After discussing the issue, we came to the agreement that it was only fair to require all of our children to abide by the same curfew. Even though we had been raised differently, we came to the decision jointly. Likewise, you and your coparent may have different points of view while talking about issues behind closed doors, but when a decision is reached, you must be united in that decision.

Do Not Be a "Wait Until Your Father Gets Home" Disciplinarian

Way too often, I have been witness to friends and family members raising their kids with the "wait until your father gets home" threat to keep them in line. Do not be that mom, whether the threat refers to your husband or another coparent. On the other hand, you may be the stricter parent, and your husband or coparent may be the one uttering that phrase or something similar. Either way, that should not be the message given to the children.

When I was growing up, my dad traveled for work often and was not around much through the week. My mom tried to hold down the fort, work a full-time job, and go to school for her master's degree in the evenings. In addition, there were family members trying to second-guess her responses because of our unique family situation, in which she had stepped in to raise us after my first mom died. As my siblings and I grew into teenagers, some more rebellious than others, my mom sometimes felt overwhelmed in trying to discipline us, and in her frustration she would say, "When your father gets home, he is going to hear about this."

When my dad got home, my mom would fill him in, and we would get the lecture about what we had done wrong and what the punishment would be. The problem was that by the time my dad got home and could lecture us, it was days past the incident. Since he was not aware firsthand of what had happened, he would discipline us, but his discipline might not be appropriate or logical.

When I was raising my children, I found myself in a similar situation since my husband's typical workweek required constant travel. He would leave Monday morning and come back on Thursday night. I knew I could not be the "wait until your father gets home" kind of mom. If I had been that mom, my children would have been horribly misbehaved. If my response always had been, "You disobeyed me. That was inappropriate behavior. Now wait until your father gets home to be disciplined," I would have been seen as a very weak parent. As moms, you have to be strong in your discipline. Your children need to know that you will discipline when appropriate and when needed.

In addition to making you look weak, a "wait until your father gets home" response is unfair to the father or other coparent, who is then expected to get home and discipline after the fact. It sets up a difficult situation if that parent is seen as the only one who can discipline. In my case, I became fearful of my father because I saw him only in a disciplinary role and did not get to see him as a fun-loving dad spending time with his children in other ways.

Your children need to know that they will be disciplined by whichever parent is with them at the time. Present a united front, where both you and your coparent will be on the same page and will discipline your children when necessary and appropriate. Your children should not be waiting until another parent is available to be disciplined.

On-the-Spot Decisions

You cannot plan for everything, and there will be times when you or your coparent will have to make on-the-spot decisions when it comes to your children. When that happens, you and your coparent have to support the decisions made by the other. Even if it is not what you would have done, you must support the decision. Later, you can have a discussion behind closed doors and say, "If that situation comes up again, I would prefer that we address it this way."

If your coparent had to make an on-the-spot decision, you have to support that decision so that your children are given the gift of a united front. The united front is what your children need to see. For example, after your coparent responded in a certain way, the child may come to you, saying, "Dad said I could not go to Carol's house to study. He said I needed to stay home and study on my own." Even if you would have responded differently and don't agree with the decision, your response has to be something like "Your father has already told you his decision; that is your answer."

Children love to go to both parents with a request, hoping that at least one of them will give them the answer they want. That is why this united front is crucial. Without it, your children will learn to ask the parent they feel will be more lenient on an issue.

If my children went to my husband, who they felt was the more lenient parent, his first response would be "Have you asked your mother about this?"—especially if he knew it was an issue on which I would likely respond differently than he would. If they said no, he would say, "Then you need to talk to your mother about it and see what she says." If he thought the issue was one that I would feel more strongly about, he might say, "Whatever her decision is will be fine with me."

If they said, "Yes, and Mom said I can't go to the party at Sam's house this weekend," his response would be "Then you got your answer." He would support my decision.

If your children ask your permission to do something, you might ask, "Have you asked your father?" If they say no, you can respond on the spot if you feel comfortable doing that. If you think your husband would want a discussion about it, then you might reply, "I will talk to your father about it and let you know what we decide." You have a few options in your response if they have not yet asked the other parent. If, however, your children have talked to the other parent, have been given an answer, and are then coming to you in hopes of a different response, you must support the decision of the other parent.

Your children need parents who are in control of raising them, parents who communicate with each other and respect each other. They need their parents to present a united front, and in order to effectively do that, you and your coparent must communicate with each other. Children may not appreciate it at the time, especially when they get an answer they do not want, but when they get older, they will understand why you did what you did.

Children need to be held to certain expectations. Whatever those expectations are, determined by you and your coparent, the children must be held to those. There has to be consistency in those expectations, so make sure you and your coparent are on the same page. That way, every time a specific issue comes up, your children will have a reasonable idea of what that expectation is. The expectations will be that consistent.

Communicate with Your Coparent to Make This Work

In order to present a united front and make this gift work for your children, you have to communicate. This is crucial. If you and your coparent are not communicating, your kids will know you are not communicating. They will manipulate you and your coparent to get what they want. Adults must be in charge here, not the children through manipulation. Your foundational principles of child-rearing will be communicated to your children. In how you respond to discipline, to the issues that arise, and to the difficulties that your children have, you will be communicating those principles, and they need to be consistent. Discuss with each other when questions, situations, or issues arise.

If you have to make an on-the-spot decision that might conflict with the wishes of your coparent, make sure you communicate afterward, explaining why you had to respond as you did. Adjust if you need to for future questions along those same lines. You are coparenting your children, and you want to stay focused on what is in the best interests of your children.

You may not get along with each other if you are not living together. Maybe you are not married to one another, maybe your relationship is strained, or maybe there were some difficulties in splitting from each other. No matter the issues between you and your coparent, when raising your children and communicating about your children, stay focused on what is in the best interests of your children.

My mom died tragically when I was very young, and my dad remarried shortly after that. There were quite a few negative relationships between my maternal grandparents and my dad and his new wife. My siblings and I were able to figure out very quickly that there was not a united front because the adults in our lives were not on the best terms with each other. If we were staying with our grandparents, we knew that they would sometimes let us do things that our parents would not allow.

Love your children enough to respect your coparent. When you decide things together and present that united front, you love your children in the most important way you can, by communicating with their coparent and presenting that united front. That will keep you and your coparent in charge. As the adults, you should be the ones in charge. This gift of the united front will help you in raising healthy, well-adjusted, and secure children.

Chapter Eight
The Gift of Family Traditions

Those who have a strong sense of love and
belonging have the courage to be imperfect.
—Brené Brown

Children Want to Belong

At the core of every child is a need to belong to something. Traditions remind your children that they share something special as a family; traditions help build family bonds. When your children experience a rough patch, those family traditions remind them of a family foundation, and that centers them. Family traditions instill in your children that desired sense of belonging. Children who do not have a feeling of belonging in their family will look for it elsewhere. That might mean getting in with the wrong crowd, succumbing to peer pressure, or joining a gang—all because they have a desire to belong. By creating strong family traditions, you are giving your children a strong sense of belonging within your family.

How I Recognized the Importance of Traditions

When I was raising our children, there were many family traditions that we started with our children or continued from our own families. I wanted traditions to bond our family together, but I never really knew the importance of those family traditions to my children until they got old enough to tell me how important they were.

As they grew, I loved hearing them fondly recall our family traditions and reminisce about those times with each other. As I listened to those conversations, I recognized that all of those traditions had such a strong purpose, such a significant meaning in the lives of our children. I began to think about that every time we shared a tradition together; each one bonded our family even closer together and further secured our love for each other.

When you have family traditions in place, they serve as a reminder to your children that they have something special. Even if they find a similar tradition in a friend's family, that does not diminish the power of the tradition within their own family. The tradition will remain special to your children because it represents family bonds and time spent together with the ones they love.

Sharing traditions makes you realize the value in them. When you hear about the traditions of other families, you realize the importance of them, and you might want to try something similar in your own family. To give you some ideas, I will share some of the traditions in my family. You might want to change or tweak one (or more) of these to make it your own. These are all so special within my family, and I hope they will inspire you to create traditions within your family.

Birthdays

In our family as the children were growing up, birthdays were a big deal. When it was your birthday, it was *your* day. It was the one day when I could devote special time and attention to one child and that attention was accepted by all. The other children would not be upset about it because they knew that when it was their birthday, the same attention would be showered on them.

When my children were growing up, I wanted to be the first one to celebrate their birthday with them each year. I wanted to do that first thing as they awoke, to send the message *Today is your birthday. It is your special day, so we will make a big deal out of it from the very beginning.* I began thinking about a way to do that when they were very little, and I created the doughnut party.

Either the night before a birthday or early the morning of the birthday, depending on where we were living and how far away the doughnut shop was, I would make a secret trip to get the doughnuts. If I got them at night, I made the trip after my children were in bed so they would not see the doughnut box. If I bought them in the morning, I would get up early and be back before they were awake. Even though the birthday child always knew that a doughnut party was coming, I still tried to keep it as much of a surprise as possible.

On the birthday morning, everybody would wake up early—parents and siblings. Extra time was built into the day so that we would have time for the doughnut party. Our children, my husband, and I would all gather around the breakfast table. All eyes watched as the birthday candles were placed in a doughnut, one for each year of the birthday child's age, and the candles were lit. As I carried that doughnut with the flaming candles to place before the birthday child, we all sang "Happy Birthday" as a family. The birthday child then got to open his or her birthday gifts from Mom and Dad, his or her siblings, and other family members. After the doughnut party, everyone would get ready for the day and head off to work or school.

Some of my favorite photos of my children are those taken at the doughnut parties—sleepy-eyed children with bed head and morning faces sitting around the table, eating their doughnuts with chocolate on their lips and joy in their hearts. Never once was there a complaint about getting up early to celebrate somebody's birthday doughnut party. No one was ever upset about losing those few minutes of sleep.

When everyone got home from work or school, the birthday child got to choose his or her favorite restaurant, and that is where we would go for dinner. Again, there were no complaints from others. If the birthday child chose restaurant X, and one of my other children hated that restaurant, everyone still had to go because the birthday child was empowered that day to make the decision.

As we ate dinner together at the birthday child's favorite place, we would continue the celebration, listening to birthday stories from the school day, sharing conversation as only a family can, and wrapping up the final part of the birthday child's special day. Even today, if we are together for birthdays, we continue that tradition. My children are at the ages now where it is not often that we get to be together for their birthdays. Sometimes it works out for my youngest child because she has a summer birthday. Sometimes it works out for my oldest child because her birthday falls around Thanksgiving. My son's birthday is at the end of September, so we are not always together for his birthday, but we all find time to call each other and wish the birthday child a special day.

Birthdays were a big deal when I was growing up too. We did not celebrate to the same extent as I did with my children, but we did always have a cake and a birthday party of some kind, and the child was celebrated. My husband's family did not make such a big deal of birthdays. When we married, my husband was not used to a big celebration even for his own birthday.

We raised our children to look forward to birthdays because I wanted to have that family tradition. It was a big deal in the sense of family bonding. It was not a big deal in the sense that the gifts were big and extravagant; we did what we could afford. But it was their day to shine and have special attention showered on them.

Family Vacations

If we had time off, we spent it as a family. That was important to us. I was a stay-at-home mom until our youngest child was in elementary school; my husband traveled. I had time off, of course, because I was at home raising the kids, but my husband was limited in his vacation time.

If he had time off, we would plan a vacation so we could strengthen our bond as a family. I cannot remember my husband and me going away just the two of us on vacation. I do remember a few times when my husband had conventions or award trips on which I might accompany him without the children because these were employee-and-spouse-only situations. When it was vacation time, we spent that time as a family. We would think about new things that we could do together that everyone in the family could enjoy.

When our children were in middle school and learning French, we decided to vacation in Montreal, Canada, so that our children could practice speaking French. We could not afford to vacation in Paris, but we were living fairly close to Canada, so we experienced Montreal as a family. We went to art museums, the underground mall, and unique restaurants and experienced so many different things as a family.

Once in casual conversation, a friend mentioned how beautiful Maine was in September. Since Labor Day weekend was only a few weeks away, we decided to head to Maine for a family vacation. We were living only a few hours from Maine at that time, which made for easy access. We spent a long weekend together as a family in Maine, walking around the quaint town of Ogunquit. We walked along beautiful cliffs, and our kids were excited to be at a beach, even though the ocean water in September was freezing. We still laugh about how the kids went running into the water, not knowing it would be so cold, and how we waited on a trolley that never came to pick us up—because, we finally realized, we were waiting on the wrong side of the street. Even now, that trip to Maine is remembered fondly by the whole family.

We often took vacations that required long trips in the car, and to this day, my children find long car rides relaxing. My daughter Meghan often wants to plan a summer road trip with me, even as adults, since we both have time off in the summers. You would be amazed at what wonderful conversations can be had with your children on road trips!

Family vacations together do not have to be extravagant. The point is spending that time together and experiencing new things together. When our children were in college, my husband's job required a move to South Carolina. We were waiting on our house to sell in Iowa while we were living in South Carolina, so my husband's company was paying for our temporary living in an apartment.

We were still living in that small two-bedroom, two-bath apartment, waiting for our house to sell, as Christmas quickly approached. My husband and I were thinking, *What in the world are we going to do with our entire family home for Christmas in this small apartment?* Luckily, in all of my husband's travels, he had saved up hotel points, and we realized the balance was very large.

We decided to spend Christmas in New York City that year. When we told our children, they were thrilled. We had never done that before—spent Christmas at a destination other than the location of family we visited. That Christmas, however, it was an option for us since we could stay for free in a New York City hotel and stay with family members along the way from South Carolina to New York City.

All the presents were wrapped and loaded in the car; they had to be stashed in all kinds of crevices and under seats. When we arrived at the hotel in New York City, the bellman came over to the car to help with luggage and watched in surprise as I pulled present after present out of the car. I had counted the presents as they were loaded into the car, so I knew how many had to come out. As the bellman and my husband helped get the presents out of the car, I counted them to make sure we had retrieved every single one, and they all made it into the hotel.

When we are home on Christmas morning, part of our tradition is having breakfast together, and we didn't want that to change just because we were away from home. Luckily, many places were still open on Christmas morning, and my husband made trips to Starbucks and McDonald's to bring back breakfast before we opened gifts. Since it was not something that happened all the time, it is still a very fond memory for us all.

Family vacations have always brought us such joy that even though my kids are now adults, we try to get together for family vacations whenever we can. Last summer, we planned a summer trip, but my son's medical school schedule prevented him from joining us. As we stopped to take pictures at one of the tourist attractions, Mary Kate said, "I don't want to take photos because Matt is not here. It just doesn't feel right."

Our family vacations have been such a bonding experience that when we've had to take a vacation without one of our family members, everybody has been a little sad. Do not pass up opportunities to take those family vacations together. Even if it is only a long weekend or a staycation, take the time to make those memories.

When we were living in Connecticut, we decided one autumn to take our own fall foliage tour. We drove from Newtown to Kent, in awe of the beautiful colors as we traveled. We stopped the car in Kent and took a walk through the fall leaves, along the rocks, and up and down the hills. It takes only a little imagination to plan some unforgettable family vacations, and they don't have to be extravagant to be remembered long after the vacation is over.

Thanksgiving

For the longest time after my husband and I got married and when our children were little, we rotated our holidays. We would spend Thanksgiving with my family and Christmas with his family, and then the next year we would reverse it. Once our children got old enough that we could not keep Santa Claus alive and be gone for Christmas, we started having Christmas at home and visiting family a day or two after Christmas. Over time, people's schedules changed, and family members became more unavailable.

Several years ago, we went to Louisiana for Thanksgiving, which is where my husband's family lives, and a new tradition began. We decided that all the girls in the family were going Black Friday shopping, getting up very early or staying up very late, depending on when the stores opened. We even added a late-night/early-morning trip to IHOP as part of the Black Friday tradition. Since we are usually together for several days before Thanksgiving, the girls traditionally have lunch together before the holiday at one of our favorite places. The boys in the family did not want to be left out, so they arranged a barbecue lunch tradition for themselves. Those Thanksgiving food favorites that are unique to our family always show up on the menu, as well as those favorites that my children have loved since childhood, and every year there is a fight over the green bean casserole.

Our Thanksgivings in Louisiana are family bonding times and have become so special within our family that the holiday has its own name. Since my children's names as well as the names of their cousins all start with M, this holiday is referred to as the M. Bartow Thanksgiving. From the time it ends one year, we count the days until it begins again the next year.

Christmas

In our family, we love holidays and the family traditions that go along with them. From the earliest days with our children, Christmas has provided one of the best opportunities to create family traditions. One of the things I did from the time my children were small was dress them in fancy holiday attire and take Christmas photos in front of the Christmas tree. I would take several pictures and pick one of those to be the photo on the Christmas card.

When my children were teenagers, they would say, "Oh, Mom, do we have to take that picture in front of the tree again?"

Of course, I would answer, "Yes, you do!"

Even though they might have sighed and rolled their eyes, every year they wanted to see how the photos turned out, and they would offer their input on which picture they preferred as the picture that would make it onto the card. About a year ago, we even took out all the photos that we had taken through the years, and everyone laughed, reminisced, and commented on how everyone had grown through the years.

Another thing I started when my children were younger was the Christmas letter. I would write a letter to our family and friends sharing the highlights of our year and tuck it inside the Christmas cards. It was time-consuming for me, especially at the busy holiday, so I had to carve out time to write it. I never was sure how that family letter was received, until last Christmas.

My children were in their twenties, and I thought it might be time to discontinue the Christmas letter. I started to tell a few people that I would not be writing the Christmas letter that year. I was amazed at the dismay that I heard from family and friends and the pleas to keep it going. "No, but we want you to write your Christmas letter! You have to do it; we look forward to that every year."

Since it was Mary Kate's last year in undergrad, I decided to write it one more year. This would be the perfect closing-out time, I felt. I was at peace with my decision, but it was still so heartwarming to hear that something I had spent a considerable amount of time writing every year was treasured by so many.

Every year that I wrote a Christmas letter, my children could not wait for it to be finished so they could read the paragraph about them and the highlights of their year. The other gift that came from that annual Christmas photo and letter is that they provided an annual family history. I have saved every photo and letter in a folder; I can read through them and reminisce about the past accomplishments and interests of my children. Those photos provide visual documentation of how my children have grown from year to year. Those are priceless traditions that I am so glad I took the time to start when they were little.

Christmas Eve traditions are some of my favorite ones. We always dress up and attend Christmas Eve Mass together; as a Catholic family that is important to us. Afterward, we head to a restaurant to eat breakfast for dinner, since there is nothing else open at that hour with the early holiday closings.

When we get home from dinner, the children get to open one present from under the tree. From the time they were little, that one present has been Christmas pajamas. In the early stages of the tradition, I was even sewing those Christmas pajamas. When I did not have time to sew them any longer, I would search the stores to find them matching pajamas. When they outgrew wanting to match, they still wanted their holiday pajamas, and I made sure they had them to open on Christmas Eve. Over the years, my husband and I even joined in the Christmas pj's tradition. Even though they are no longer children and they know what is beneath the wrapping paper, they still get excited about opening that one gift on Christmas Eve.

Each year, as we settle around the TV in our Christmas pajamas, watching *It's a Wonderful Life* and eating Cyclops cookies fresh from the oven, we are bonded together in a heartwarming and loving experience. I recognize in those moments that traditions do mean something. When our children are grown and they still want to continue traditions started in their childhood, it means something.

When my children were in upper elementary school, they created their own Christmas Eve tradition of sleeping in the den, camped out together, so they could wake up and head downstairs together on Christmas morning. These were moments of sharing their lives together as they fell asleep at night. For us as parents, it was so wonderful hearing those Christmas-morning footsteps as our children bounded down the stairs, ready to take on Christmas morning together.

When my children were little, the anticipation of opening gifts drove them to get up very early. Since my husband and I didn't want them up too early, usually because we would be up late filling stockings and putting together toys and bikes, we would say, "If you wake up before 7:00 a.m., just go back to sleep."

We put clocks in their room so they knew what time it was. When they would wake up and realize it was after seven o'clock, they would run into our room to wake us up. If they woke up before 7:00 a.m., they would either go back to sleep or chat together with giggles and whispers. When we are all together at Christmas today, everyone prefers to sleep late. They laugh about those early years and say, "Remember how we would wake up on Christmas morning, look at the clock, and wait? Then the second the clock struck seven, we would run to wake up Mom and Dad." Even that became a treasured memory for the kids.

To help our children get in the Christmas spirit, we always had them exchange gifts with each other. The gifts could be handmade or simple. The important thing was that they were taking time to think about their siblings and taking the time to shop for them or make something. Even today as adults, they will decide ahead of time the budget for buying gifts that particular year for each other, and they still carry on that tradition of exchanging gifts at Christmas.

One of the other crucial things they did for each other related to Santa. As Meghan and Matthew reached the ages where they recognized Santa was not real, they still worked so hard to keep Santa alive for their younger sibling or siblings. Meghan helped keep Santa alive for Matthew and Mary Kate. When Matthew realized Santa wasn't real, he helped keep Santa alive for Mary Kate. The older children found great joy in keeping Santa alive for their younger siblings.

Importance Carries into Adulthood

With my children now adults, all those family traditions that we started when they were younger are still treasured. They have carried those traditions into adulthood with them. We often laugh about the idea of them still liking to do their Christmas Eve campout in the den together and have those nightly conversations before Christmas morning. We laugh about what will happen when they have spouses: how will that work out?

Even when my children are together for birthdays, they take part in those birthday traditions with each other. They look forward to when we can all be together as a family, even though we are all spread out and must work harder to get our schedules to mesh. I recognize the importance of all the traditions that were created as I was raising my children when, even as adults, my children want to carry those on with each other.

Your Own Traditions

Think about the family traditions that you have; think about what a gift they are to your children. Maybe you can identify areas where you want to create more family traditions. Maybe you can find even more time during which your family can bond through family traditions. If you do not have traditions right now, you can always add them. It is never too late.

Some of the traditions that we have in our family have been created in just the last few years. The idea is just that once you start them, you continue doing them. You can start now, no matter what age your children are, and those traditions will carry on with them for years to come.

Children will look back on those traditions with so much fondness and so much love. They are a reminder of their family, of how they fit together, and of how special their own family is. These are gifts that will last a lifetime for your children. Indeed, they may last for generations because your children likely will continue quite a few of the traditions, if not all of them, with their own children. Then their children will share those traditions with their families.

As a mom, you are the one who must create those family traditions and give that gift to your children. You are the one to start those traditions that will carry on and bring happiness and a sense of belonging and unity to your family for generations. Create unique family traditions for your children, keeping in mind what works best for your family. Those traditions will be treasured for years to come because traditions provide priceless family moments.

Chapter Nine
The Gift of Faith

*Your greatest contribution to the
kingdom of God may not be something
you do, but someone you raise.*
—Andy Stanley

Religion and Spirituality Define Us

Our religion and spirituality are parts of us that help define who we are. They are integral parts of our being, and they are a very personal part of us. No matter the religion or the depth of spirituality that you have, faith is important to give your children.

Faith reminds your children that they cannot always be in control. It reminds them that they are not the center of the universe. It reminds them that there is a higher power always there for them and looking out for them. They can look to this power for guidance, help, and support in troubling times.

No one's life journey is easy from start to finish. Everyone faces times of challenge and difficulty. A life without trial or tribulation will not happen. It helps to know that there is something greater, the higher power that is God, helping you through your life. Children need that sense of well-being that comes from faith in God.

People without Faith

Meghan had a friend in college named Abigail. She worried about this friend and felt bad for her because Abigail did not believe in God. Whenever things went wrong in Abigail's life, she would get very depressed because, in her mind, there was no way out. Her thought process was that this was life, this was what life had given to her, and there was nothing she could do about it.

Abigail did not have the faith that would lead her to think that maybe this was a lesson she needed to learn and God would help her through it or that maybe this was a test for her, but she would be stronger when she got through it. She didn't have the faith necessary to think that she could pray about her difficulties and God would give her strength because He had a plan in mind for her. She did not have the ability to reason in that way because she did not have faith. When bad things happened to Abigail, they really brought her down because she could not see the higher purpose. She had a negative personality because of that lack of faith.

Abigail saw how my daughter responded when faced with challenges and said, "How do you have such a positive attitude, even when you are facing really difficult things?" It was because of my daughter's faith. As someone without that, however, Abigail could not understand where that strength and peace could come from.

When my children were young, we had neighbors who would adamantly tell me that they did not believe in God, and they were actively teaching their children that there was no God. I was saddened by that. If you have come to that decision as an adult, you have made that conscious choice for yourself, but when you instill in your children the belief that there is no God, you are not allowing them to find their own beliefs. When you take away that gift of faith, the gift of knowing that

God is there for them, you are setting them up to have more difficulties while working through life's tragedies.

Even when your children have blessings in their lives, feeling grateful and recognizing that those are blessings from God can have a positive effect on their perception of their world. If you are struggling with your own faith as you are raising your children, embrace the idea that children have a way of drawing you closer to God. Child-rearing can provide wonderful opportunities for strengthening your own faith. Children have a way of making us recognize the miracles all around us because they often vocalize their awe of God's handiwork as they explore nature and the world around them. Share those awe-inspired moments with your children. You will be giving that gift to them even as you are finding that gift yourself.

How Can This Benefit Them?

How does belief in God benefit your children? When I was a very young child, I experienced an extreme tragedy with the death of my mom. Not much can be more traumatic to a child than losing her mom. Your mom is everything in your young life, and when you lose her, it can make you feel that the world is not a good place. My grandmother was able to break the news of my mom's death in such a way that, despite the extreme sadness, I was able to process it, grieve, and cope, knowing that my mother's love would always be with me.

My grandmother told me that my mom was with God in heaven, but she would always be with me and watching over me. As I grew, I did feel she was there watching over me. When difficult things happened, I knew not only that God was there but also that I had my mom as a guardian angel watching over me. Just knowing that helped me get through that tragic point in my life.

Yes, my mother was no longer physically with me, but I knew that her spirit would remain with me and watch over me.

I am so thankful that my grandmother was able to present my mother's death to me in such a way that I was able to recognize God's presence in my life. God would still be there for me even though I was dealing with something so difficult.

When a child recognizes that God has a plan, then adversity does not have the same negative influence. If you have faith that God will help you through the challenges and that God has a plan for your life, when you experience adversity, you will be able to face it, work through it, and grow as a result. That turns a negative experience into something positive. Growth is always a positive thing.

When you have faith, you know God is looking out for your world. You can make a difference—and your children can make a difference—simply by praying. Bad things will still happen because evil exists in the world, but your children will have faith that good will ultimately triumph, and that will give them the needed strength to deal with the difficulties and tragedies in life.

My favorite picture as a child hung in my grandmother's living room. It was a picture of Jesus knocking on the door of someone's house. It was titled *The Unexpected Visitor*. I would look at that picture, at the kind, loving face of Jesus, and feel peace. As a child, it was powerful for me to know that Jesus had lived as a human and experienced very human things and yet had such an unfailing faith in God.

If you are not sure of God yourself, please consider exposing your children to God and letting them decide, rather than taking something away that could positively impact their lives. As moms, you make sacrifices for your children all the time because you want the best for them. Even if religion and spirituality are not things you feel comfortable with, they have the potential to be a powerful gift for your children.

How to Instill Faith in Children

Faith can be instilled in your children in a variety of ways. If you regularly attend church, take your children with you so they can experience public worship and see you giving your adoration to God. Talk about God and talk to God in their presence.

Be open and specific when sharing your faith with your children. When raising my children, I shared with them if I was working through a challenge and asking for God's help. "I was really struggling with our upcoming move and choice of schools. I prayed about it, and God answered my prayers by helping me feel peace about our decision."

I frequently told my children that they were blessings in my life and that I was so grateful to God for each one of them. I talked about how God had seen me through difficult events, I prayed with them and for them, and I shared with them the many times I had relied on God throughout my own life. Anything you do to show that God is an integral part of your daily life will help instill faith in your children.

When you talk about God in the presence of your children, you are sharing your faith with them. That sets a powerful example. Your children will learn that God is there for them because God is there for you.

Even when I had difficult times with my children, when they were pushing my buttons and stressing me, my children would hear me start to pray, "God grant me the serenity ..." My kids knew I was at my wit's end at that moment because I was saying that prayer. They saw that even in those moments, I was turning to God and asking his help to guide me through a difficult situation.

Pray as a family. Pray together before you have your meals, pray before your children leave for school, and pray together at night. Prayer was a part of the bedtime ritual with my own children. I would tuck them in, ask them the daily question, and pray with them. When they grew to an age where they preferred to pray alone after I tucked them in, I never left their room without saying, "Remember to say your prayers."

Speak about God in natural conversation. Make God an ever-present part of your lives by speaking to God and about God. As my children were growing up and facing challenges, I would say to them, "Do your best, and I will say a prayer for you." If they were traveling, I would tell them, "While you are gone, I will pray that you have safe travels." Let your children know you are praying for them each and every day.

Encourage your children to get involved in church if they can. Your children will grow closer to God when they are involved in faith-filled activities. Whether they attend youth group, help at Sunday school, or sing in the choir, these opportunities will help develop faith in your children.

Encourage your children to help the less fortunate whenever they can, whether through collecting food for a food bank, distributing blankets and clothes to the homeless, sending cards to those serving in the military, visiting the sick, or raising money for a particular cause. Your children will be serving as instruments of God, and their own faith will be strengthened in the process.

Demonstrate values that God has instilled in you, and you will instill faith in your children by example. Volunteer in your own right, go to church, pray, and ask for God's help and protection in the presence of your children. Thank God whenever your prayers are answered, and let your children hear you thank Him. By doing these things, you are showing your children that God is an essential part of your life.

You Are Your Child's First Introduction to God

As moms, you are everything to your children. You are the first one who shows them love, protection, security, caring, and family. When you demonstrate all those things, you are doing for them just what God does for you. You are exemplifying God in the way you mother and nurture your children.

You are *the* most important person to your children. Show your children that as strong as you are in their eyes, you still look to God when you are facing difficult things. You praise Him and still look to Him for guidance and protection.

Even when you are disciplining your children, keep God and their souls in mind. Disciplining children is not just about making sure that they are behaving appropriately here on Earth but is also about helping them make choices that will be good for their souls. When my children were confiding in me about challenges and difficulties, I would give them comfort; I would give them advice and then always say, "Pray about it, and I will pray for you too."

My children got the message *I will help you, and I will guide you, but you need to get God involved, and you need to pray about this. I will pray for you too.* My children grew up knowing that God was important to me, and I always hoped that they would see that God was active in their lives too.

I Grew Up Knowing the Importance of Faith

In my immediate family, we did not go to church on a regular basis, but I did grow up knowing about God. I would see my mom pray, and when I visited my grandparents, I would go to church with them. I heard them talk about the importance of God; I heard and felt that spirituality from both my mom and my grandmother.

I recognized that they looked to God and that He was important in their lives. I saw my mom read the Bible, and she said prayers with me, and whenever my grandmother called me or wrote to me, she always reminded me that I was in her prayers. When my grandmother explained to me about my mom's death, she made sure that I knew my mom was happy and safe with God in heaven. That gave me comfort.

I grew up secure in life even though I knew firsthand that bad things could happen. I was able to move past the loss of my mom because I knew about God, I knew He was there for me, I knew my mom was watching over me, and I knew there was a purpose in my life. With that faith, I knew I was going to get through even the most difficult things that life could bring.

Baptismal Birthdays and Other Religious Holidays

You should celebrate not only your children's birthdays but also other religious holidays as a way of developing your children's faith. For my children, not only did we celebrate their birthdays—those were the big celebrations—but also there was a tiny celebration on each child's baptismal birthday. I would honor their baptismal birthdays by giving them a religious gift to remind them that their baptismal birthday was an important milestone in their faith life. If there are religious holidays that you celebrate, take advantage of those opportunities to strengthen your children's faith.

In our Catholic tradition, the saints have their own feast days. I could not possibly celebrate every feast day, but I picked the ones that are important to me such as St. Patrick's Day because I am of Irish descent, St. Valentine's Day because the children were celebrating that anyway, and St. Nicholas's Day as part of advent. On those days, I would give my children cards and little gifts. It was another reminder that these celebrations were part of our faith.

Each religion has its own sacraments and celebrations. Whichever ones are celebrated in your church, make them special days with your children. Each celebration represents a step forward that your children have taken in their faith life. Celebrate with them and remind them that those celebrations are important. Every time you remind your children about those special days, you strengthen a connection to their faith.

Communicate to Children That You Are Praying for Them

While raising my children, I reminded them that I was praying for them on a regular basis, and I still do so to this day. Every night, I pray for them. When they are experiencing difficulties, I pray for them. When they are at turning points in their lives and trying to work through critical choices, I pray for them. When situations arise, they know that my prayers will be added to theirs. Communicate to your children what your prayer life is.

Communicating to your children when prayers are answered is crucial for building faith. When a child experiences the answer to a prayer, it builds his or her faith. Help your children to remember that when they ask for things in prayer and those prayers are answered, they need to thank God for that.

Communicate the importance of trusting in God's will. We do not always get what we are praying for because God knows what we really need. I would remind my children that if their prayers were not answered, what they had prayed for was not meant to be, or it just wasn't time yet. God's timing is more perfect than anything we can hope for. I frequently told them, "Everything happens for a reason."

One of my favorite songs is "Unanswered Prayers" by Garth Brooks. There are times when you think you want something, you think you need something, and you pray about it, but it just does not happen. Then you realize a week, a year, or even several years later that there was a reason that the prayer was not answered. God knew better, and you thank God that He did not answer that prayer.

Is the Faith Still There as They Grow?

You can do everything to instill faith in your children—you can work to build that faith day by day and year by year as you are raising your children—but still you may wonder whether you did enough to instill faith in your children and ensure that they carry that with them as they grow up.

Your children may get to a point where they question their faith. In the middle-school years, the teen years, or young adult years, they may question their faith. If you raised them knowing God, and you did everything you could to instill faith in your children, be patient. *Be patient.* Know that they will ultimately find their way back. You just have to trust in it, pray about it, and wait.

My son may not vocalize his faith in God often, but if I see him grab a scapular before boarding a plane, I know that faith is there. If I see my youngest daughter struggling through a challenge, and she has her rosary next to her bed or in her hand, I know that I instilled faith in her. When I hear my oldest daughter talk about getting involved at church and attending Mass each Sunday, I know that I have instilled that faith in her.

Pray for your children, and allow God to help them find their faith. Even if they are questioning their faith, even if they are going through a period where they are not practicing their faith as much as you would like, trust that you did everything that you could. Trust that God will help them to find their way back. Sometimes, it is the children who question their faith and ask those tough questions that end up being the strongest in their faith as adults.

God Is Always There

Teaching your children that God is always there is a crucial part of instilling faith in them. Even when your children seem like they are testing their faith, they know God is there if you have instilled that faith in them. My children know this. They know God loves them unconditionally, expects them to lead a good life, and will be there when they falter. If you are instilling faith in your children, your children will have those same guiding beliefs in their lives.

Your children will be tested in life; mine certainly have been. My children have endured job losses, family deaths, difficult consequences, and dangerous situations. My son has battled cancer, and my youngest daughter has survived an abusive relationship. They have made mistakes, faced the consequences, and taken steps to correct them. Every single time they were tested, they knew that God was there for them. That gave them the strength they needed to get through the sadness, uncertainty, and fear.

You cannot always be around to guide them, but God can. Instill that faith in your children. Children need the gift of faith so that they know that something greater than them, God, is looking out for them and wanting the best for them every day of their lives.

Chapter Ten
The Gift of Open Dialogue

The way we talk to our children
becomes their inner voice.
—Peggy O'Mara

Set the Stage at the Earliest Moment

Set the stage for open dialogue at the earliest moment with your children so it feels natural and grows and develops over time. If you want your children to come to you as teenagers and young adults when they are struggling with problems that have the potential to seriously impact their lives, set the precedent at the youngest age that they can come to you about anything and you will listen. More than any other person in their lives, you will have their best interests at heart. That is what moms do.

You are the best person for them to come to with problems or when they just need to talk to someone. However, you might find it uncomfortable to have conversations about difficult topics, especially if you are uncertain about how best to respond. It can be unnerving and unsettling, but don't let those feelings take over. Focus on getting outside of that discomfort so you can be there for your children. Keep the focus on allowing the conversation to flow. Let your children know you are there for them, you will listen, and even if it is something uncomfortable for you, you want them to come to you and share with you. Every time your children come to you to talk and they are heard, it strengthens your relationship and will lead to deeper conversations later on.

No Topic Off-Limits

Communicate to your children the message that no matter what the topic is, that topic will never be off-limits for discussion with you. As my children were growing, I made time to listen to their questions and remained open to whatever it was that they needed to talk about. I provided insight on what they were contemplating, offered a safe place for them to talk about it, and offered an explanation when that was what they were looking for.

If a sensitive topic arises in a place where it cannot be discussed, let your children know that it *is* a good question and you want to talk with them about it, but now is just not a good time or place. Stress to them that you want to talk about it in a private place when you have time you can devote to the conversation. By so doing, you will let your children know that you understand the importance of the topic and of talking through it together. You are not putting off the question or making them think it is something they cannot discuss with you.

Never dismiss a question that your child brings to you or avoid an opportunity for discussion. If your child comes to you needing to discuss something, or your child comes to you with a question, do not put it off unnecessarily, do not dismiss it, and do not avoid having that discussion. If your children bring something to you, they need you to talk to them about it. If you dismiss that question, you will make them feel like it is not a valuable topic to discuss with you, and you never want them to get that message.

Conversations with my children have ranged from heartwarming to difficult to sad to funny. Conversations that you have with your children will encompass all of these emotions as well. No matter the frame of reference for the question or discussion, whether you will be sad, heart-warmed, embarrassed, nervous, or challenged, take the time to have that conversation with your child.

No matter what the topic is, you have a chance to learn something about your child in that discussion. You have the opportunity to provide him or her comfort, assurance, and an explanation, and who better than you to do that. You are the best person because you are Mom. Show your child you will be there, no matter what.

They Will Not Always Get the Answer They Want

When my children came to me with questions or things they wanted to talk about, I listened, but I could not always change the situation they were facing. Even though I could not always make the pain or the struggle go away, I could listen to them and give them an opportunity to voice their concerns. That was sometimes all they needed because it allowed them to feel better and understand what they needed to do next, and it gave them clarity and confidence in their abilities to get past the struggle.

Put yourself in a similar situation for a moment. When you have something that is concerning you, even if someone cannot fix it for you, you feel better when there is someone you can talk to about it. Just having a sounding board can help you through that situation. It is the same with your children. They feel better knowing that you will listen to them, genuinely hear them, and give them a chance to voice their concerns. That is helpful even when you cannot completely make the situation better for them.

When my children came to me with difficult things, by listening and talking to them, I was able to lessen the stress they were feeling. Just being able to talk through difficulties with someone else relieves stress and clears a person's mind to see the possible solutions, and your own children need you for just that. Just as you feel better talking to someone when you are facing challenges and frustrations, your children feel better after talking to you.

When my son was being bullied in elementary school, he shared that with me as we were sitting on the floor in his room, playing with his toy trains. The bullying was in its early stages, and he felt safe bringing it up to me in conversation. I helped him think through some actions he could take that might lessen the problem, and I was able to provide some insight to help him understand that the problem was not with him, but with the bullies. I also made sure he knew that if the problem continued, he had to let me know.

When my oldest daughter came home after struggling as a waitress, she used me as a sounding board. We talked through what her options were and what path to take; that helped her find a solution. When my youngest daughter was struggling in a relationship and wanted to end her engagement, she grappled with how to communicate her decision to other people. She talked through the situation with me, and I helped her just by listening and giving her a chance to formulate her next steps.

Difficult Discussions

Some of the discussions your children need to have with you will be difficult for you. The topic might make you feel sad or uncomfortable. The topic might give you pause as to how best to respond. Don't let these feelings keep you from those conversations.

When my grandmother died, my oldest daughter was only three years old. I had to explain to her about death and what had happened to her great-grandmother, and I provided comfort in her grief. I helped her understand how God fit into life and death so she would not be fearful living her life. When my husband's career aspirations took us on move after move as we were raising our children, I had to be open to listening to how sad the children were to leave their friends, how angry they were that this was happening, and how concerned they were about making new friends and fitting in. Those were difficult conversations, but I had to be available to them, help them cope with the changes, and give them ideas for how to work through the experience.

When one of my husband's job changes led us to move from Connecticut to Florida, we had to find someone to keep our family dog for a few months. We were in temporary living while waiting for our house to sell, and dogs were not allowed. Temporary living went on longer than anticipated, and the person keeping our dog no longer could keep her. We suddenly had no choice but to give away our dog permanently, and we worked hard to make sure we found her a loving home. My children were frustrated and very sad. As difficult as it was because I hated seeing them upset, I listened to their frustrations and sadness, did my best to comfort them, and helped them understand that we had done everything we could to make sure Belle was in a good home with people who would love and appreciate her.

When our local parish priest was arrested for arranging to meet a young teen for sex, I was shocked. My children had interacted with him many times since they were active in our church and parish school; the potential heartbreak that might come from having that conversation with my children was terrifying. I was so afraid of what I might hear, so afraid that they might tell me something inappropriate had happened. I knew, though, that I had to give them the ability to share with me if that was the case, so that we could get them the help they needed.

Fortunately, nothing inappropriate had happened with my kids. *Thank God.* I do believe that the priest was not able to take advantage of them because of the open dialogue I had established with my children from the very beginning. They knew about stranger danger; they knew that the private parts of their bodies were off-limits to others. I had prepared them for the fact that there were people in the world who would not look out for their best interests. It was because of this that I was able to breathe a sigh of relief after asking them about interactions with that priest. I was so thankful that they had their wits about them enough to keep themselves out of a situation that could have been tragic.

If I had discovered that the worst had happened, I would have provided a safe place for them to talk through it and let them know that it was not their fault. I would have done whatever was necessary to help them cope with it. Your children must know that you are going to be there for them even in the most difficult situations or conversations and that they can rely on you to help them get through the struggle.

Examples of Conversations

The conversations you will have with your children as you are raising them will run the gamut of possible topics. Consider these opportunities to talk about topics that will impact them and help them make good decisions. Take the time to have those discussions whether they are about friendships, problems they are having at school, problems they are having with particular teachers, or problems they are having in the family.

As they get older, peer pressure will become a topic. If you have created an atmosphere of open dialogue, they will tell you what their friends are doing and what they feel they are being pressured to do, such as underage drinking and sex. Be in the frame of mind that you will welcome those discussions, even if the topics are unnerving and uncomfortable for you.

As their mom, you need to allow those topics to be brought to you. My thinking was always that if they were not talking to me about those topics, then who would they be talking to? If I was not the one giving them the answers, then I might not like the answers they were getting. I welcomed the fact that they were coming to me because there would be no question about the answers they were getting.

So Important, Especially for the Discussion of Sex

Open dialogue is so important, especially when it comes to the topic of sex. It is hard to accept sometimes that your children will reach an age where they will start thinking about sex. You start out with precious little babies, and it is hard to foresee the peer pressure they will be exposed to as they grow and mature. As you are raising your children, you will think, *They are my babies, so how can they possibly be old enough to be thinking about that?* The truth is, they know about sex—and usually long before their parents think that they do. I have seen this as an educator and as a parent. That conversation among peers comes up at a very young age and much sooner than most moms anticipate.

When you are raising your children from the earliest age, remember that their private body parts have real names. Just like an arm is an arm, a leg is a leg, a vagina is a vagina, and a penis is a penis. They need to hear those words and hear them used correctly. When you give nicknames to those body parts instead, your children get the message from an early age that there must be something wrong with those body parts if they cannot even call them by their real names. An additional benefit to doing this is that you will become comfortable with those names as well. This will benefit you when the conversations about sex come up as they get older.

As your children reach puberty, they experience so many changes in their bodies. By the time they reach that age, they should have already had conversations with you about sex and other sensitive topics, so that they will not be afraid or embarrassed to talk to you as they are becoming so self-aware and self-conscious. If that open dialogue has been the norm from the earliest moment, of course they will come and talk to you because that relationship has already been established.

When I was a very young girl, I heard about a distant cousin whose mother had never told her what menstruation was. When she went to the restroom one day and saw the blood, she became hysterical, thinking that something was terribly wrong. It was actually my great-grandfather who was present and who had to be the one to tell her that this was a part of life, a very natural thing. How embarrassing and scary for that young girl! She was afraid of something that was normal simply because her mother had been afraid to talk to her about it.

Talk to your children about the changes that they will experience at puberty: hair growth, change in voice for boys, periods and growing breasts for girls, and the moods and emotions. Prepare them before they get there. Let them know these changes are natural and signal that they are growing into young men and women. This is a change that they should see and experience as a positive rather than negative change.

When I was in junior high school, my friends and I would sit together as a group at recess and talk about what was going on in our lives, bonding and sharing as only friends can do. One day the discussion about how we first had been told about sex came up. I could not really recall one particular conversation that I'd had with my mom. I just remembered that from an early age, I had known about sex, and I was comfortable with that knowledge.

One of my friends shared with us that her mom had just recently handed her a book, told her to read it, and advised her to ask if she had any questions. I knew my friend was not going to ask her mom any questions after reading that book. Her mother was trying to do the right thing. She probably thought this was the proper time to educate her daughter about sex, but since there had never been an ongoing dialogue between my friend and her mom, I knew that after reading that book, my friend would not feel comfortable asking any further questions of her mother.

Power through any discomfort or embarrassment that you may feel about discussing sex and other topics with your children, and start early. When your children are young, the conversations will not need to be as in-depth because you will be answering the questions they ask. The conversations will progressively get more difficult as they get older, but you will be more comfortable with the subject by then.

Do not delay the conversation. What is the most difficult will also provide the greatest opportunity to bond. That pertains to ongoing conversations on all important topics but especially on the subject of sex. For a lot of parents, sex is the most difficult subject, but that first conversation about sex is a milestone for your children and provides a tremendous chance to bond with them.

Children are usually embarrassed to talk about sensitive topics with others, but if you open up that dialogue early in their life, they will talk to you about these subjects when they are older. You will be seen as the one they can trust since you have been honest all along, you have not avoided any conversations with them, and you have been willing to listen, whether they were providing information about situations or sharing their opinions.

Never put that trust in jeopardy; treasure it. They need to know that if they come to you with anything, you will listen to their opinion, give advice, and help guide them in the right direction. Most importantly, you will provide a good sounding board and a chance to talk about what is on their minds and in their hearts.

When raising my children, I had an idea about the time frame in which I would tell my children about sex based on what I had read from the experts and what I had experienced in my own life. I was waiting for a telling question to come forth because that would be the signal that they were ready. Your children will guide you and let you know when they are ready for certain information. If you have raised them in an atmosphere of open dialogue, they will come to you with a question when they are ready to learn about the topic. When that happens, the best way to handle it is to answer the specific question with an age-appropriate response. If they ask another question on top of that, and if they comprehend what you are telling them, then give them more information.

My daughter Meghan was finishing up first grade when she first asked a question that related to sex. Her little sister was more than a year old, and she asked, "How are babies made? Where do they come from?" I answered her question, and she followed it with more questions. At that early age, she learned that when a mom and dad love each other very much and decide they want a baby, there is a physical act of love. The dad's penis goes into the mom's vagina, an egg is fertilized, a baby is created, and the baby grows in the mom's uterus until it is time for it to be born.

She sat there and listened, her eyes got a little wide, and it set in that this was the truth. The stork does not deliver babies; no babies are left on doorsteps. I specifically told her that this was not a topic she could discuss with any of her friends or siblings because this was a private conversation that children should have with their moms or dads. I let her know that I was telling her because she was old enough to ask the question, and I wanted her to have the correct information. She kept the information private and did not tell her siblings. I knew this because when they were about the same age, they each came to me with the same questions.

Even though some might think first grade is too young, if your children are old enough to ask the questions, they are old enough to be told the truth. Mine were asking, and I didn't want them learning about sex from someone else. I would not know what information or misinformation they were receiving. Meghan (and later, her siblings) came to me with a question, and I answered the question. Additional questions followed, and I knew that I had to provide the correct information.

The questions were getting deep enough that if I had lied to Meghan and told her something just to get out of the conversation, then I would have been doing her a disservice. Since I listened and answered her questions with information she could understand, it created a bond. Even at that young age, she never felt like she could not come to me with questions. That open dialogue continued with my son and my youngest daughter as well.

Moms Can Have the Conversation with Sons

Through the years, I have heard friends and family members say that they will have the conversation about sex with their daughters, but they are not having that conversation with their sons. They are going to let their children's fathers do that. That may make sense to you too. You may be more comfortable with your sons getting that information from their dad, but my husband was extremely uncomfortable having that conversation with our son. He was actually dreading it. To add to the scenario, my husband traveled a lot of the time. Since we do not always know when those questions are going to be asked, I discussed the issue with my husband beforehand, and we both agreed that I would field the question.

When my son was around the same age my oldest daughter was when she asked, he started asking the same questions. I was the one who was present when the question came up, and I was the one who was comfortable answering it. I had already had this same conversation three years earlier with his older sister. Even though it was a little different talking to my son, discussing the process of how babies are conceived and the love that should be involved in the process was the same. The additional questions were unique to each child, but at that point, I was providing the information as asked.

Looking back, I am so glad that it ended up the way it did and that I was the one who told my son. That created a bond that continued. Throughout his life, he has always felt comfortable talking to me about sensitive topics without embarrassment. As a woman, I could provide a unique perspective that he never would have heard from his dad. Even though you do not have the same body parts as your sons, you know the importance of them hearing the correct information. If you are the one having that conversation with your son, it will create a powerful bond because your sons will think, *Mom is the one I have been talking with all along, so why should I feel uncomfortable going to her now?*

As moms, you are the best ones to educate your children, even your sons. With all of your children, push through your own discomfort and embarrassment and engage your children in those critical conversations. You will have their best interests at heart and will make sure they get the right information.

Sex Cannot Be a One-Time Conversation

The whole point of this gift of open dialogue is that it is continual and ongoing throughout the lives of your children. Especially with the topic of sex, dialogue cannot mean a one-time conversation. Like the case of my childhood friend who was just handed a book by her mom, there are not going to be any questions from your children about sex if there is not an open and ongoing dialogue. From that very first moment that I had a conversation about sex with my children when they asked that first question, I never even considered that I would never have to talk about sex again. Of course, I would have to talk about it again. What you say to a child when he or she is six years old is different from what you will say to the child when he

184

or she is eight, ten, twelve, or fifteen years old. The conversation is constantly ongoing and evolving. As your children grow older and are able to hear additional information, you must be the one to provide that needed information.

Part of the sex conversation must include telling them about inappropriate touching. This is critical. If I had not told my children about this at a young age so that they knew to be aware and come to me if anyone ever tried to touch them inappropriately, then I would not have been comfortable talking with my children about the incident with the local priest. My children were spared from inappropriate touching and what could have been an even worse situation because they already knew the potential dangers. They knew what inappropriate behaviors were, and that kept them from getting into a situation that easily could have taken a bad turn.

As my children grew, the conversations evolved to what they most needed to hear at the time. We had conversations about STDs, HIV, and pregnancy. We talked about pregnancy prevention and the importance of abstinence. Those conversations came when my children were ready and the time was right for them. That open dialogue had been the norm since the earliest moments, so when it was time to have those discussions, we were all open and ready.

Sometimes those conversations were initiated by my children based on what they were hearing from friends. Sometimes I initiated those conversations myself. Your children are yours to raise and protect, and you are the one who should provide the information so that they can make educated decisions. When you hold back information—for example, maybe you do not want to tell them about STDs or HIV or pregnancy—then you are putting them in danger. They will certainly hear about these things, be exposed to them, or be caught in a situation where someone takes advantage of them in the worst way. Give your children the information so they can protect themselves.

If your children have heard about sex from you, if they have been told about what dangers are out there, if you have guided them with your advice, and if you have provided sound reasoning for why something should or should not be done, they will listen to you. They will trust you and will know that you have given them the right answers when they have asked. That will help them make the right decisions.

Some parents think, *If my kids know about sex, then my kids will actively engage in sex.* That is not true. Knowing about sex will not make your child have sex. Other factors will impact that decision; the knowledge alone will not make that happen. Knowledge, however, does have the potential to keep them from being sexually active too soon, and knowledge definitely can help prevent pregnancy. Knowledge will give your children the information they need to make educated decisions about sex, abstinence, and pregnancy prevention.

Kids are having sex at younger and younger ages. That is a scary thought, but it is happening. You do not have the luxury of waiting until your children are in middle school to tell them about sex. If you wait until middle school, the odds are they will already have friends talking about it and doing it, and your children will be hearing the wrong information. Answer their questions truthfully when they start asking at the youngest age.

Recognize that although you will educate your children about sex and hope that they will choose not to be sexually active, even good kids will choose to have sex before they are ready for it. Even if you have given them all the right information, even if you have advised them to wait until they are married or at least until they are in a committed relationship (whatever the value is that you wish to guide your children to), your teenagers still might choose to be sexually active. If that does happen and they come to you, they will be comfortable talking with you about that decision because of the precedent of open dialogue you will have set.

You may tell them that you think they should wait because they are not emotionally ready for sex, or you may help them to see that it is not the right time for them even if their friends are telling them it is. You can tell them what precautions to take if that is what is needed. Several years ago, I read a magazine interview with an Olympic athlete. He had been proactive about HIV and safe sex, and he said, "As much as parents would like to think it is not going to happen, if kids want to have sex, they are going to have sex."

If you turn a blind eye, thinking you cannot say anything to your children because you worry that will make them go have sex, your worry is misplaced. You need to educate them, help them see that the best choice is to wait, and give them the reasons why. Then recognize that when they become teenagers, they still might choose to be sexually active. You need to be the one to provide the education about sex and help them make the best choice for them.

When I was a teenager, I had a friend who had never been told about sex. She was in high school and dating a young man who was about a year older than she was. They had been seriously dating for a while. One day, she came to her friends in tears and panic. She thought she was pregnant from an encounter with her boyfriend.

As she continued to explain what had happened, with her friends asking questions for clarification, it became clear that my friend and her boyfriend had not had sex. They had been making out on the couch, hot and heavy but fully clothed. Still, she thought she had become pregnant from that encounter. She was in high school, yet no one had ever taken the time to tell her about sex. She did not have the information she needed to know how a girl does in fact get pregnant. I felt so sorry for her; her friends had to tell her that her makeout session could not have gotten her pregnant. She should have heard that from her mom—and long before high school.

If They Can Trust You to Listen and Answer, They Will Come to You

Your children are always learning, from the moment they come into this world; they are sponges and soak up every bit of knowledge to which they are exposed. If they have questions, you are the one who provides answers. You want them to grow up to be good people and contributing members of society who make good choices and have a good life. You want them to feel comfortable coming to you and starting conversations about topics that they need your insight about. Give them that guidance and that open dialogue.

Too many of my friends and family members have waited until middle school or later to have discussions with their children about sex. That is too late. Have that conversation earlier with your children. You have to be seen as the one they can trust, the one who will give them answers, and the one who will listen. Even as they grow older and make their own decisions, they will still remember the advice that you gave them. Even if they make a mistake, even if they do something wrong, they will feel like they can still come to you and you will guide them to work through it. Provide that information. Be their trusted advisor and begin open dialogue at an early age. It is such a profound gift.

Chapter Eleven
The Gift of Love of Learning

Children are made readers in
the laps of their parents.
—Emilie Buchwald

Reading from Infancy

Children learn to read in the laps of their parents—how true that is. From the earliest moment, if you are taking the time to read to your children, that is a profound learning opportunity for them and such a special time for you.

Reading from infancy was something I felt strongly about with my own children, understanding its impact. When I found out I was pregnant with my first child, I joined a children's book club right away. Books were sent to me on a regular schedule, and I was accumulating them in a little library for my daughter before she was even born.

Once Meghan was born, I began reading to her, even when she was just an infant. I wanted to start that habit early. Many of these times, she was not able to keep her eyes open. She certainly was not looking at the book, but she was hearing me read to her. I believed that my spoken words would be soothing and that being close to me would create good memories. Reading would be thought of in a favorable light.

Reading to my daughter was a wonderful bonding time between us. As my other children arrived, reading to them was a special bonding time too. My reading to them from the earliest days helped my children think of reading as a positive activity. When my children were old enough to sit in my lap or side by side with me in a chair, I continued to read to them every day. Reading a few books together became part of our bedtime ritual.

Reading also became the perfect waiting-in-line activity, and you can incorporate reading moments in that way too. Prepare your children for waiting in line or waiting at a doctor's office and have them bring some books to read. If you want to keep your children quiet in church or at a restaurant, reading serves as a quiet yet engaging activity. Books are better than any electronic device.

Reading exposes children to vocabulary, and eventually, they learn how the reading process takes place. In the first stages, you are reading to them, and they are just hearing the words. Then they start to notice that you are looking at the page, and as they get older, you can even put your finger on the words as you read. They will make the connection between those symbols on the page and the sounds you are making.

Since reading was part of our bedtime ritual, each child had favorite books that she or he would request. Meghan's favorite was *George's Store*. When we asked her at night which three books she wanted us to read, *George's Store* was always one of them. We read it so often that she had the book memorized. She was not reading the book, but she had heard the words enough to memorize them. Eventually, she did learn to look at the letters that made the words, and she learned to read.

Meghan was on the fast track with language acquisition. Since she was the first child and I was a stay-at-home mom, I had a lot of time to read to her. Reading became her favorite activity, and she was speaking in small sentences at an early age. I did not put too much thought into what I was doing that might be impacting this quick language acquisition, until she was about eighteen months old.

Meghan was in her car seat riding in the car with me when we passed the convenience store QuikTrip, which had a logo of two letters. Meghan pointed at the sign and said, "QT." In that moment, I realized she knew some letters, maybe just those two, and I wanted to find out whether she knew any others. As soon as we got home, I began showing her different letters and asking her to identify them. To my surprise, she knew all of the letters of the alphabet!

I had never sat down with her and said, "This is an A; this is a B; this is a C." Still, there she was at eighteen months old, able to recognize the entire alphabet. One of her favorite books at the time was *ABC* by Dr. Seuss. Just from my reading that book to her on a regular basis, she had learned all of her letters. She was a little sponge, soaking up everything.

When Meghan was about two years old, my husband was awarded a trip from his employer for his outstanding sales. My grandmother was happy to care for my daughter while we were away. Since Meghan had to have books with her everywhere she went, I took a stack of books to my grandmother's house, knowing that Meghan would want my grandmother to read to her.

When my husband and I returned from our trip, my grandmother said to me, "Oh my goodness! I was reading to Meghan one night when I stopped reading because she seemed more interested in drawing. She looked up at me and said, 'Read, Great-Gran. Read.'"

Meghan loved when others read to her, and she was not going to let Great-Gran off the hook. If you are reading to your children, you are exposing them to language, and they will learn to read when they are developmentally ready.

How to Incorporate Learning
into Everyday Activities

You can do many activities that your children will see as fun and games but that also will provide opportunities for your children to learn. Read to your children, and let them see you read. Whether it is a magazine or a book, let them see you read. It is important to model that for them.

My first teaching assignment was in a classroom of first graders, and I was lucky to get that spot. I had been a teacher's aide in the elementary school for a couple of years and was taking courses to get my teacher certification. In this new school year after only three weeks, the teacher left. The school was in a bind; it had a classroom of students but no teacher for them. The school was able to get permission for me to teach the class since it was an emergency situation, the children knew me, the parents requested that I take over the class, and I was working toward my certification at the time.

I was a little worried, thinking about the magnitude of the assignment. First grade is the year in which children learn to read, and I would be the one teaching them. I had thirty-three first graders (and their parents) depending on me to make sure they could read by the end of the school year. I did what I knew, what I had learned, and what I had done with all three of my children. Every morning started with a morning message that I had written for them on the easel of chart paper. My students would gather around in circle time, and I would read the message, pointing to the words as I read.

Certain words and phrases such as *you, we, and, the,* and *good morning* were frequently repeated in the morning message, and my students began to recognize these words, even out of context. I provided a print-rich environment; everything in the room had a label with the word identifying it. If they looked up at the clock, they saw the word *clock.* If they looked at the chalkboard, they saw the word *chalkboard.* I read "big books" to them, putting the books on an easel so the children could see them. I did everything I thought might help and put everything I was learning in my college courses into that classroom. By the end of that school year, every single one of those children could read. I was so grateful; that had been my mission.

Even at home, read to your children and point to the words as you read to them. Let them see you write. Write messages to them and point out the words as you read the messages. Create a print-rich environment, even in their bedrooms, by labeling items so they can clearly see the words associated with those items. At the grocery store, you can help them pick out items by symbols or logos when they are first starting and then move to picking out items by letters. All this exposure will help them learn to read.

Talk to them about where items come from. When you are getting the milk, talk about cows and farms. Do the same in the produce section. Talk about where the vegetables and fruits come from and the process of how they get to the grocery store.

As they get older, you can ask them to look at two jars of peanut butter and determine which one is cheaper. Help them learn to calculate the unit price. Let them organize the cart, putting all frozen foods in one place or everything that begins with a C in one area, whatever is age-appropriate for them.

Teach them about reading nutrition labels. Ask them if the item has a lot of sugar or sodium. Ask them if they see healthy ingredients such as calcium or protein. If they cannot read a lot of the words, you can read the label to them. "This says it has nine grams of sugar. Is that good or not?" Start at an early age, and later they will be able to read those words and figure those things out for themselves.

Educational activities during time spent in the car provide wonderful learning opportunities. If your children know the letters of the alphabet, you can ask them to look for a certain street by telling them what beginning letter to look for on the street sign. If they can read, they can be even more helpful.

Help them learn directions by asking them to help you with turns. "At the next street, I need to turn right. Which way is right?" You can play the license plate game on long trips by looking for letters in order on license plates.

The car is also a great place to have conversations since your children cannot get out or walk away. If there is something you want to talk to them about or you want them to learn about, have that conversation with them in the car. These conversations are also bonding opportunities.

Keep the car stocked with books for your children. In the early stages, they may just be looking at the books. As your children learn to read, they can read those books to you in the car. That time will allow for necessary reading practice.

The kitchen can also be a place of learning. If you are cooking or baking, your children can look at the recipe with you. As they get older, they can help you measure things out, which provides math practice with fractions and units. Put alphabet magnets on your refrigerator. While you are attending to your kitchen duties, your children can be spelling words on the refrigerator. In the early stages, your children may just be playing with the letters, and you will be the one spelling words. Even if they do not know what the letters are yet, they are seeing the letters and learning to associate them with words.

Cooking and baking also provide opportune conversation moments. You can have those conversations while your children are on the floor playing a game, sitting at the counter drawing, or reorganizing cabinets for you. These activities can give you time to have those conversations while they feel close to you. Sensitive topics won't seem so overwhelming in moments such as these.

Do You Know Matthew Can Read?

I exposed all my children to books at the youngest ages, but I never formally sat down and taught my children to read.

Instead, I talked to them and read to them frequently. I let them see me read, and I helped them write their names.

When my son was in preschool, I went to pick him up one day, and the teacher said to me, "Do you know that Matthew can read?"

I had to laugh, and I responded that yes, I knew that. She told me how he had plopped himself down on the floor, taken out a book, and started reading that book out loud. "He is only four years old," she noted.

All I had done was expose him to letters, read to him on a regular basis, and provide a print-rich environment. When he was developmentally ready, he learned to read.

Mary Kate Preferred Other Activities

With my first two children, I exposed them to language and reading, and they learned to read on their own when they were preschoolers. Even though my youngest child did not like reading, she did let me read to her. When it came to choosing her own activities, she preferred hands-on activities over reading.

Mary Kate liked to have her hands in some concoction, creating something rather than holding a book. Still, she was introduced to reading in the same manner as her siblings. I read to her on a regular basis; she had the same exposure to language. Even though reading was not her favorite activity, she still learned to read on her own before she was ever taught to read in school.

When Mary Kate became a middle-school student, she began to enjoy reading. She found a particular series of books that intrigued her. She recognized that if there was a particular book that interested her, she loved to read. She would read a huge book for hours on end and get through it as quickly as she could because she loved the book and wanted to move on to the next book in the series.

The payoff will come if you keep reading to your children, no matter whether reading is a favorite activity or not. If you continue to expose them to books and language, when they are developmentally ready, they will learn to read. Mary Kate became an excellent reader, just like her siblings, even though it was not her favorite thing to do.

My Early Years

When I was growing up, my mom was a schoolteacher. I would see her doing activities such as reading and putting time and effort into education. She exposed us to books and learning at home. I witnessed my dad studying for different degrees that he wanted to achieve in his field.

I have an early memory of a time when we had just moved to a new house across town. My mom was in the kitchen unpacking dishes and organizing cabinets. My sister and I were on the floor playing with letters, doing puzzles, and looking at books. These were activities that were helping us learn.

Many memories were made with me sitting in my mom's lap while she pointed to the words as she read to me. I was making language connections in those moments, realizing that she was pointing to words because they meant something. From those cherished moments, I developed my own love of reading.

Education was important in my family, so I grew up loving learning. When I started school, my sister was younger, of course, and was not in school yet. The first thing I would do with my sister when I came home from school was play school with her. Anything I learned that day in school, I taught her.

My sister sat through playing school at a young age because I wanted to teach her. That helped her when she got to school on her own. She was ahead of the game because she had been practicing with her big sister for years.

Reading was one of my favorite activities. I loved to read, I treasured books, and I read with excitement. A family that lived up the street had two children who were a bit younger than I was. The mom would ask me to come and read to her kids. She told my mom how much she loved for me to read to her children because I read with such animation and excitement in my voice. Even though I was only nine, this mom appreciated how I read with feeling and passion.

Because I had always loved learning, I wanted to instill that in my own children. Create that love of learning in your children by making everyday activities opportunities to learn. Read, read, and read even more; read to your children from the earliest age.

Vocabulary

I have always loved words, and because of that, I have a large vocabulary. The words I use might not be the words others would use, but I am comfortable with them because they long ago became part of my everyday vocabulary. These are customary words for me regardless of when or to whom I am speaking.

When I was raising my children, I did not adjust that vocabulary. I did not think I needed to baby-down my vocabulary because I had young children in the house. The way I normally speak is the way I spoke to my children. If I was using a word that they did not understand, I didn't refrain from using the word. I just used the word normally and then explained what it meant.

My children grew up not only hearing my vocabulary but also learning that if they heard a word that was unfamiliar to them, they could learn what it meant. Over time, as they heard the word over and over, it became part of their vocabulary too.

Avoid using baby talk with your children as much as you can. When your children are babies, of course you will coo back to them as they coo to you. You will be so enamored with the children with whom you have been blessed and with those precious first sounds and words they make. As your children grow, talk to them in a normal voice with your regular adult vocabulary. If you just baby-talk to your children, they will not be exposed to richer vocabulary, and they will not get the chance to make that vocabulary part of their own.

When I was pregnant with my second child, Meghan asked about the baby one day while we were shopping. She referred to the baby as being in "Mommy's stomach." I replied, "The baby is growing in Mommy's uterus, and in a few months it will be fully grown and ready to be born."

Even though Meghan was very young, I used the correct word: uterus. I did not want her to think that a baby grew in someone's stomach. The stomach is part of the digestive system, not the reproductive system. After I used the word, I explained that the uterus is a special place that moms have where babies can grow and develop until they are ready to be born. She heard the word and its meaning.

When Matthew was about five years old, we were invited to a birthday party for one of his friends. Other friends and their families were there to celebrate too. My children and I had just been served our cake when my son walked up to one of the adults serving and asked, "Do you have any utensils?"

Two older girls standing behind me heard my son's request, and one said, "Utensils? He knows the word *utensils*?"

My son used that word because it was part of his vocabulary, even at five years old. It was a word that I used often and interchanged with *forks, knives,* and *spoons.* He had learned the word because he had heard me use the word in context.

When I was teaching middle school, I mentioned something about a rhetorical question one day in class. My students had never heard the word *rhetorical,* and they asked what it meant. I answered, "A rhetorical question is not meant to be answered."

They fell in love with that word. Sometimes when I would ask a question, they would joke with me and ask, "Mrs. Bartow, is that a rhetorical question?"

Another word I used with my students to strengthen academic vocabulary was the word *assessment*. Teacher colleagues told me that they never used this term; they just used the word *test*. But *assessment* was part of my vocabulary, so that is the word I used with my students.

Vocabulary acquisition improves reading comprehension. When children are exposed to rich academic vocabulary at a young age, it becomes part of their own language. The benefits of a large vocabulary continue throughout their academic careers. The richer their vocabulary, the better children tend to perform on standardized tests.

Provide the print-rich environment, use your adult and academic vocabulary, and avoid baby talk. Think about those words that you normally use, and recognize that you may need to explain what certain words mean, but over time, your children will understand those words, which will become part of their vocabulary.

What Meghan Sees

Meghan is now a school psychologist, and she evaluates children who are struggling in school to determine what the issues might be. She decides whether interventions are needed, or if interventions have already been tried without success, she might test the child to see whether the child qualifies for special education services. One day when she was doing her graduate work and practicing interventions with students who were struggling, she called me to say, "Mom, thank you so much for reading to me when I was a child because today I worked with a little girl who is struggling in school. She has no disabilities that would cause the struggle; the only reason she is struggling is that no one is reading to her at home."

This child was fully capable of success in school but had not been exposed to reading. Meghan created reading interventions for the child because the child's home environment was not providing those opportunities. Once the interventions were in place, the child made quick progress.

You cannot expect that loving your children and spending time with them will be enough to provide a foundation of learning. You cannot expect to send your children to school and have the teachers provide their entire foundation of learning. If you are not providing that foundation of learning—instilling a love of learning in your children from an early age, practicing skills with them, using strong vocabulary, having everyday learning activities with them, and providing a print-rich environment—then you are sending your children off to school at a disadvantage.

All of those years when your children are sponges, soaking it all up? If you neglect those years by not providing everyday learning opportunities, your children will likely be lacking in foundational skills when they start school. Whatever you can do, do it. Do not worry if you don't have a lot of money to provide opportunities. Opportunities to learn abound in everyday activities. You are going to the grocery store anyway; use that as a learning opportunity. You can go to the library and borrow books; you do not need to buy them.

One of my children's favorite activities when they were younger was going to the public library. We would go to the library on a weekly basis and pick out books. We would keep them all week long, reading them as many times as my children wanted. Then we would head back to the library and pick out a whole new set of books for the next week. I never would have been able to buy all those books for our home library.

You can ensure that your children will be successful in school before they even get there by creating everyday opportunities to enrich their learning. My daughter Meghan noticed that once she created interventions for struggling students and put them in place, those children made very quick progress. It was not that the children had disabilities; they just had never been exposed to language, reading, and learning opportunities.

When the home environments provided this exposure, the children excelled. Use that knowledge to create a learning environment and a love of learning for your children.

What Are Refrigerator Letter Magnets?

A few years ago, I encountered a family at my school in which all the children were delayed developmentally. The children were not acquiring language, and many other essential skills were lacking. A colleague of mine who was certified in special education sat down with the mom to figure out what the mom was doing at home to help her children learn. In the discussion, my colleague discovered that there was not much going on at home and the home environment was not a learning-rich environment.

When my colleague asked whether the mom had refrigerator letter magnets, the mom replied, "What are those?"

This mom had not thought about or researched the many ways she could help her children learn at home. Because of that, her children were not being exposed to important opportunities to learn, and many were already in school and struggling.

My colleague explained what refrigerator letter magnets were and helped the mom devise some activities she could do at home with her children. Some of the children were not even in school yet, so they would have that learning environment before they ever got to school. The school-age children would also benefit from those extra learning opportunities while at home.

When thinking about what you can do with your children, remember that it is not about the money you have, but about the exposure to language, reading, math, and essential skills. Be creative with providing learning opportunities. You can expose your children to learning in a number of ways no matter what your financial means are.

Trips to Montreal

I was always looking for ways to help my children learn. My husband and I did not have a lot of money; I was a stay-at-home mom, and we had made a lot of sacrifices in order for me to be able to do that. When my children were learning French in school, we wanted to provide an opportunity for them to practice that language. As mentioned earlier, we did not have the means to take our family of five to Paris, but we did have enough to drive to Montreal, Canada, so that they could practice their language skills.

We prepared the children before we went by telling them this was an opportunity to practice their language. We told them that when we got to Montreal, we wanted them to speak in French to as many people as they could. When we went into a restaurant, the servers would begin to speak in English or first would ask if we spoke English. We would ask the servers to speak in French even though my husband and I were not fluent in French, in the hope that our children would be able to translate for us. The waiters and waitresses would come up to the table and speak in French; our children would respond in French. While we were out and about in Montreal, we had our children read the French signs for us and read the menus if they were printed in French.

That trip provided an opportunity for us to show our children that what they were learning in school was important to us. We wanted them to get a message: *You are learning French, and we want you to use that French. We treasure this new language you are acquiring, so we will provide this opportunity for you to put that into practice.* Think about things that your children are learning and ways that you can show them that you appreciate what they are learning. Help them put what they are learning into practice as often as you can.

Allow Children to Try New Things

Exposure is a wonderful way for your children to learn new things. Even if an activity is something that they choose not to stick with long-term, they will learn something just by trying an activity. Your children can take that knowledge and expand their intellectual foundation.

Provide opportunities for your children to learn, and recognize that these opportunities do not have to be lifetime missions. Maybe just in that moment, that month, or that season, they will enjoy the new activity; they certainly do not have to be great at it. After trying a new activity, your children might decide they do not want to continue pursuing it. The goal is to expose them to different activities to provide learning opportunities, not to put pressure on them to excel at these activities.

My older children usually had a pretty good idea of what extracurricular activities they would enjoy before they started them. Because of that, they would usually stick with an activity for a long period. My youngest, on the other hand, would get an idea of an activity, try it, realize she didn't enjoy it, and want to move on. I did not want to raise Mary Kate to think it was appropriate to quit on things. At the same time, I wanted her to recognize that it was fine to try many different things.

When Mary Kate was in fourth grade, she wanted to try Irish dance. I had to pay in eight-week increments, so I told her that she would have to stick with it for eight weeks, and then we could decide whether she wanted to continue. She did it for eight weeks and decided it was not her thing. Throughout her life, Mary Kate would get interested in an activity and ask to try it. I would give her a time frame that she had to commit to the activity, and that worked to provide the balance between commitment and "sampling" things.

If someone is moving around from activity to activity, that person can be seen as a quitter. Mary Kate hated that assumption. When Mary Kate was in her early college years, she said, "You know, Mom, I am not a quitter. What I am is somebody who likes to experience a lot of things."

When she came to that realization, I was so proud of her not only for recognizing it but also for sharing it with me. She had been able to try so many different things, including Irish dance, police camp, basketball, softball, cheerleading, piano, show choir, and skydiving (just to name a few), and learn from each one. She had experienced them all because she was not afraid to try them. She moved on once she no longer enjoyed an activity and once our agreed-upon time commitment had been met. She might not have stuck with one thing for a long period, but that exposure was a rich experience for her.

Perfection Should Not Be the Goal

Anything your children do should never be about perfection. I am not perfect, you are not perfect, and no human being is perfect. Humanity does not come with perfection, so you must ensure that your children understand that perfection cannot be attained. Instead, send the message that you are looking for them to try their best at anything they do.

It is more empowering to instill the value of a job well done than to expect perfection. If a child feels he or she has to be perfect, that child is set up for failure right away. Perfection cannot be attained. An A is an A, whether it is a 93 percent or 100 percent. Instead of seeking perfection, encourage your children to strive to push themselves and challenge themselves. If your child really wants a 95 percent and works hard to earn it but ends up with a 93 percent, that is okay. If your child worked really hard and did everything that she could do, she can still be proud of that 93 percent, even if it was not what she was originally working to get.

Recently, I was talking to a parent of a student I taught last year. She wanted to thank me for all her son had learned from me, and she commented on how he'd really had to work in my class. She recognized the value in the effort of what her son was doing and understood that this was more important than the grade itself. She said, "Even though he got a B in your class, I would rather him have a B that he had to work for than an A that he didn't."

As an educator, I see the hazards of raising children to be perfect. These children often have anxiety issues because of perfectionist tendencies. As you raise your children to love learning, encourage them to focus on the process of learning and doing the best they can. It is not about attaining some impossible goal of perfection.

If Your Children Love Learning, They Will Learn Wherever They Are

We moved a lot when I was growing up. Sometimes, the states and school districts where we moved had really good schools; other times, that was not the case. Since I had been raised to love learning and had been exposed to educational activities at home, even when I was at those schools that were not the best, I still excelled and learned. If I was not getting it in the classroom, I was searching for it on my own. I read books, researched, or did additional educational activities to broaden my base of knowledge.

You may not live in the best school district, or your children may not have the best teacher in a particular year, but that does not mean they cannot still learn. If they love learning, they will be okay. They will get through that period. You will be enriching them at home, they will participate in educational activities that they love, and they will use their natural desire to learn to find learning opportunities on their own. Your children can be enriched outside of the classroom in many ways. If you instill that love of learning in them from the beginning, you will find things to help enrich them outside of school, and they will too.

Before my son entered medical school, he went to a small college in the South; it was the school of his choice. He then got into a top-notch medical school. His friends would tease him about the college he attended for his bachelor's degree, and he would tell them, "Spring Hill College got me to the same place as you are."

Spring Hill College was an excellent college, and my son, as well as his sisters, received a fine education there. His friends' view was that he had not gone to one of the big-name universities, so his education was not as good as theirs; that, of course, was not the case.

If your children love learning, they are going to search for knowledge. They will seek out opportunities to learn and thrive. You will have instilled in them the gift of the love of learning, and that will ensure that they continually learn no matter where they are.

Chapter Twelve
The Gift of Facing Problems and Accepting Change

Do not handicap your children by
making their lives easy.
—Robert A. Heinlein

Facing Problems Is Empowering

We are all, as human beings, going to face challenges in life. As moms, you need to let your children know that even though they will encounter problems, they cannot run from them. They must deal with them. When you teach your children to face their problems, your children learn not only that you believe in them but also that you believe in their ability to meet the challenges. Facing problems will come to be seen as a positive response.

Every time your children meet a new challenge and work through it, they get stronger. They learn to cope with adversity. They learn that even though difficult situations will arise, they have the skills to work through them. Whether those problems are academic, physical, social, behavioral, spiritual, or emotional, or anything else they might encounter while growing up, learning to deal with those problems is a necessary life skill.

In the early years, you will need to help and guide them as they face challenges. When they have a problem, you will have to help them figure out a solution. Every time you help and guide them, provide practice for them in facing those challenges. The day will come when challenges arise and they will have the skills to know how to work through them.

The ultimate goal is to teach your children how to face challenges and advocate for themselves. When they cannot advocate for themselves, the real world can be harsh and cruel. You do not want your children to face a challenge and back away from it. You do not want them to face adversity and throw up their hands in defeat. Instead, you want them to face a challenge and think, *This is going to be difficult, but I will work through it because I will grow stronger as I do. Even if it is something I have never experienced before, I am going to work through this challenge.*

When my son was being bullied, I had to help him figure out a solution. I listened as he talked through the situation. I gave him strategies to try, and I let him know that if those did not work, we would look at the next possible solution.

When Mary Kate was in second grade, she began dealing with a problem involving two of her friends. One friend became jealous and pitted the other one against my daughter. Every day, Mary Kate would get off the bus sad and tell me stories about what the other two girls were doing. I had to talk her through the situation and guide her to the solution. I asked her what she could do to change the situation. What were some things she could do to help turn the tide and put this friendship back on track? The friend that the other girl was trying to turn against my daughter started to come around when my daughter began using some of the strategies we came up with. She and my daughter actually became very good friends. The one who was trying to instigate everything was called out for it, and once she realized her efforts were to no avail, she began to back down.

When Meghan came home one day from fifth grade and told me about one of her teachers yelling at her, I asked her for the details. What had been happening in the classroom, what had she been doing, and how had the teacher responded? When I encouraged my daughter to talk about the incident, she was able to see that even though her perception originally had been that the teacher was yelling, Meghan's experience was closer to being talked to in a stern voice.

Since Meghan was rarely in trouble at school, she had perceived the situation to be harsher than it actually was. I helped my daughter think through what could be done the next time something similar happened. I asked Meghan, "If something is being said sternly and it is hurting your feelings, what can you do about it?"

This helped my daughter put the situation in the right perspective and recognize what the teacher was trying to accomplish with her stern voice. Meghan was able to determine a strategy so that the next time something similar happened, she could understand the teacher's perspective.

When I was growing up, I wanted so badly to make the dance line my sophomore year in high school. I worked really hard, went to practice every time it was scheduled, and tried my very best to make the team. However, as the selected numbers were called at the end of tryouts, I realized I had not made the team. Many of my closest friends had made the team, and I had to swallow my pride and be happy for them. I had faced challenges before in my life, and I had always worked through them.

Even though I was disappointed and sad, I knew it was not the end. I did not walk away feeling like my entire high school career would be horrible because I had not made the dance line. Instead, I got involved in an alternate activity and thought I would try again the following year. I did try out for dance line the next year as a junior, and I made the team. I made the team again as a senior. I learned an important lesson about life and how to make the best of every challenge and situation. When your children are challenged, if they work through the challenge, they will recognize that they are stronger each time.

When we moved in the middle of Mary Kate's sixth-grade year, that second half of sixth grade was very difficult for her. Getting her up every morning and dealing with her tears of sadness, knowing that she was not happy with her new school and not happy with the move, was heartbreaking for me. We had to put some strategies in place to help her through it. I helped her brainstorm things she could do at school to make friends, things she could do to find her niche, things she could do to adjust to her new teachers and expectations. I helped and guided her so she could have a successful last half of sixth grade.

When Meghan was in high school, we moved in the middle of her junior year. Meghan was so angry about it at first, but we had raised her to be able to deal with challenges. When that adversity came, even though she was angry, she was determined to make the best of the situation. She hated leaving her friends, but she believed in her ability to make new ones and have a successful last year and a half of high school at a new school in a new state.

Because of that move, which happened right as she was about to be inducted into the National Honor Society, she missed out. Her new school had already gone through the process for NHS and inducted new members. Meghan had to accept that the move had cost her something, but she had to make that sacrifice because of the needs of the family. She patiently waited, applied her senior year, and was finally inducted at her new high school.

When Matthew was in middle school, my husband was facing a job transfer. Matthew was struggling with this prospect, which led him to act out at school. I gave him time and opportunity to express his concerns. I also let him know that he would have to face this challenge but that acting out in the classroom was not the way to do it. We brainstormed ways to help him cope with the situation, and I reminded him that his father and I would do everything we could to help him transition to his new school.

Mary Kate was in show choir her sophomore year in high school and then decided to give it up while maintaining other choir activities. Show choir required a lot of travel on weekends around the state, and Mary Kate felt she would prefer having her weekends free. When her junior year started, it wasn't long before she realized that she missed show choir. She had to work really hard to get back into it for her senior year, but the time away from it had given her a new appreciation. She was challenged by the decision she had made to leave show choir, the regret she felt throughout junior year, and the wait and hard work to get back in.

As my children have grown up, they have faced breakups, illnesses, transitions, and disappointments, but every time they have faced a challenge, they have grown as individuals. This has helped to make them ready to face the next challenge and every challenge after that. Even though you will hate to see your children experience adversity and challenges, they will learn from them, and these challenges can end up being opportunities for growth. Guide your children and teach them to advocate for themselves so that as they grow up, they have skills in place that will serve them well as adults.

Matthew finally made it into medical school on his third try. He ultimately succeeded because he never gave up and did everything in his power to get accepted. Matthew never even considered a plan B. After his second year of applying without acceptance, he said to me, "Mom! I am going to get into medical school. I will keep trying until I get there because this is what I have wanted to do since I was in high school."

I was so proud of him and his determination. He was going to work through the experience of rejection; he was going to stick with his dream and work hard to make it a reality. He did, and he is thriving today because of it.

When Meghan was struggling in the nursing program at her college, she came to the realization at the end of her junior year that nursing was not for her. She made the difficult decision to switch majors for her senior year. Even with a change that late in her college career, Meghan still graduated on time, completing her bachelor's degree in four years. She was faced with a difficult decision, she rose to the challenge, and she did everything required to meet the expectation that she would graduate in four years. When your children face adversity, they are empowered to work through those challenging times. Raise them to do that.

Change Is Inevitable

Change is going to happen in your children's lives. It just will. That is what life is about. Nothing stays the same; change occurs and cannot be avoided. Your children will experience it throughout life just as you have. You can help your children accept change as something that is meant to happen, that needs to happen, and that can lead to something even better.

Instill in your children the confidence that they can deal with change and transition successfully. They will experience changes in teachers, rules, policies, schools, jobs, relationships, and homes. If they are not able to deal with those changes, then they will be at a disadvantage when they move into adulthood.

When you know a change or transition is coming, such as a family move, be honest and upfront about that change. Do not try to sugarcoat it. Let your children know that there will probably be some difficulties with the change. Assure them that you will help them as much as you can and guide them through the transition.

When my husband was downsized out of a job because his company had been purchased by another company, we had been living in the same town for almost five years. Our children were thriving at their schools, they had wonderful friends, and they were very involved in community, church, and extracurricular activities. Of course, we did not ask for my husband to be downsized out of his job, but it happened. We had to explain to our children that their dad was looking for a job and that the new job likely would take us elsewhere. When that job came and it was in a new state, they were prepared for what was to come because we had discussed the situation with them earlier.

I listened to their expressions of anger, sadness, and heartbreak. They needed to be able to express those emotions, but we also helped them recognize the strength they had inside, and we had faith in their ability to adjust and be okay. When your children are facing similar situations, help them see those personal traits that will see them through any change that they may experience.

Focus on the Positive

Anytime there is change, there will be something that comes out of it that is positive. In the moment, it might be hard to figure out what that positive might be, but there will be one. As you are talking about and helping your children deal with change, focus on the positive. For instance, if your family is facing a move, you can brainstorm with your children things that they have wanted to do but have not been able to do. Maybe the new place to which you are moving has some extracurricular activities that they have always wanted to do. Maybe it is in a nice part of the country near something that they will be able to experience on a regular basis, such as the beach or mountains.

Anytime there is a change, there is a chance to learn and experience new things. That could be part of the positive message that you give your children. For example, you might say, "This is a chance for you to learn new things. You have never been able to play lacrosse before, and now you will be able to do that."

If the change is a move or a change of schools, remind your children that the move is a chance to make new friends. You might say, "You have some wonderful friends where you are, and you can certainly keep those friends and stay in touch with those friends. Now you will be in a new place and have a chance to make even more friends."

When your children live through and work through change, it builds their character. When you are helping your children focus on the positive and recognize that this change is something they have to do, also communicate to them that you trust they will be successful, will make it through the change, and will be okay. Your children will follow your lead and the confidence you have in them. Even though it might be hard for you as their mom to see them struggle, remind yourself that this challenge will be a character-building experience and will help your children in the long run.

At the end of my sixth-grade year, my dad got a new job, and we had to move yet again, this time from the Atlanta area to a smaller city in Louisiana. We had just moved eighteen months before, so the news that we were moving again so soon was not what I wanted to hear.

My siblings and I were staying with my grandmother while my parents made the house-hunting trip to the new city. My mom called to update us on the new place. She talked about all of the positive things about where we were going to live, what our new schools were like, and what our new home was like. My favorite show at the time in reruns was *I Dream of Jeannie*, and my mom knew it. She told me, "The local television station even airs reruns of *I Dream of Jeannie*."

Bear in mind that this was in the days before cable TV. Today, you can find just about anything you want on television, but at that time, you were limited to a few local channels. I held on to that little gem of familiarity and thought, *At least when I get to my new city, I can still watch my favorite show.* If you focus on the positive, your children will pick up on the little nuggets of positivity, and those will see them through until they work through the change.

Many Moves

As a child, I moved many times. At the end of my fourth-grade year, we moved from Colorado, where I had lived for four years. I loved my friends, I loved the neighborhood, I loved my classmates, and I loved my school; still, we had to leave. My dad's job was taking us somewhere else.

When I got to my new school in Texas, things were so different than they had been in Colorado. What I found to focus on as a positive was how much I loved our new house and the many things my sister and I could do in our new neighborhood. Soon, I had a wonderful group of friends at school, I had a crush on a very cute boy, and I was feeling like I belonged. I had just qualified for the district spelling bee, and then, just six months into fifth grade, my dad's job forced another move. I was heartbroken. I did not even get to finish my spelling-bee competition.

I was so sad that I did not get to finish that spelling bee, that I had to leave my friends, and that I had to leave that cute boy who had just started to like me as well. I did not have a choice in that move; adult matters were involved, and I was a child. I had to face that challenge and find a way to cope with it, and I did.

What I learned from all of those moves as a child was that you cannot be afraid of change. Through all of those job moves, my dad was exemplifying to me that you have to go where the opportunity is. You cannot allow geography to limit the possibilities of where life might take you.

That served me well when I married a man who also was in the corporate world, a world that often equated career advancement with a job transfer. When we first got married, we were living in our hometown, a town that was not large enough to provide the career opportunities I knew he needed. My husband had finished his MBA and was working at a job selling tractors. I knew that was not the best career opportunity for him. I told him we needed to move to Dallas, explaining that he would have more opportunity and would be able to find jobs that put his MBA to good use.

Because of what I had seen as a child, I knew we needed to make the move to advance his career. I said to my husband, "We are young and newly married, and we do not have any children yet. If we are going to do this, now is the time to do it."

What a wonderful decision that turned out to be. My husband was hired by a prestigious company, and that job was the starting point for a career that has spanned decades. It was definitely the right thing to do because my husband has been able to provide for our family and at the same time enjoy the work he does. So many times, I have seen friends and family turn down opportunities because they were afraid to move. It has stifled them, hurt their careers, and hurt their families, all because they were afraid to make that change in geography.

Even though moving was a difficult thing for me as a child, I learned something valuable from each and every move. When your children experience change, they will learn something from those changes and transitions. Never underestimate the power of what they will learn and how that will apply to their adult lives.

After my husband and I started our family, we had to move many times. After we had been in Georgia for almost a decade, my husband got a job in New England. I was excited about the adventure ahead, but I was hesitant to break the news to our children. How were they going to cope with the idea of living in a little New England town?

We presented the move in a positive light and gave them as much information as we could about where we were going and what their lives would be like. As expected, they were not on board from the beginning. We allowed them to talk through their anger and frustration and explained that this was something we needed to do as a family. We trusted that they would ultimately be okay, and we helped them make that transition.

They ended up loving that small town in New England. If you asked them today where their favorite place to live was, Newtown, Connecticut, would be their choice. They thrived in that town, even though they did not want to move there at first.

Meghan had to move in the middle of her junior year. She faced it, rose to the challenge, and worked through that adversity. She got involved at her new school and in the community, she made new friends, and she thrived.

Matthew had to move immediately after he finished high school. He did not even get to enjoy the summer with his friends before everyone went off to college. We had to move, and he dealt with that adversity and ended up loving our new town. To this day, he fondly remembers those summers in the Midwest, where he spent his time working when he came home from college.

Mary Kate had to move after her freshman year of high school. She loved the high school where she had spent freshman year and hated to leave her friends. Still, she grew to love the new town and new high school where she finished those last three years. Even though she was not on board at first, she allowed herself to be open-minded, and she found happiness in her new hometown.

Your children will experience change, and most likely, the change will not be something that they are eager to face; however, when they do face the challenge and work through it, they will be able to look back and see all they have gained in the process. Help your children work through the challenge and accept the change. It is a powerful life lesson and will serve them well as adults.

Children's Perceptions

My children faced changes and obstacles as they grew, and now as adults, they are able to see those as positives in their lives. They were able to go to colleges where they knew not a soul. They knew they could meet the challenges of starting over, making friends, and adjusting to new places, and they knew they would be okay because they had done it many times before. They grew up unafraid of trying new things. They had come to learn that they could work their way through any challenge or transition; they had been challenged before and had not only survived but flourished. That empowered them even more for the subsequent challenges.

They have followed opportunities and are now spread out across the country, all in different states. They were not hindered by thinking that they needed to be right by Mom and Dad or that they needed to go someplace where they knew someone. They chose to be where they are all on their own and to create the lives they had always dreamed of having. Each one of my children can look back on every adversity, every change, and every challenge and find the positive impact.

Try not to worry when your children have changes and challenges before them. Instead, guide them and support them, but allow them to work through each experience. You cannot do that for them; they must do it. Every time they do that, they empower themselves and learn something valuable that will serve them as adults. Even when it is hard, recognize that someday this will pay off.

Living in One Place All of Your Life versus Moving

If you are able to stay in one place and raise your children there for their whole childhood, you will enjoy a situation that not many people get to experience anymore. Many great things can be said about that. Your children will maintain the same friends, and they will have memories in that house or city from the day they are born.

A few of my friends and family have been able to live in the same city or state their entire lives. They all feel very happy and lucky that they have been able to do that. I have family members who have lived in the same house from the time they were born until today. They have grown up with the same friends, attended the same schools, and worshipped at the same church and have enjoyed the perks of being able to do that.

However, if you are in a position where you do have to move, do not beat yourself up about that. Do not think that your children will have worse lives because your job or life circumstances require your family to move and experience the changes that go along with that. Yes, it can be wonderful to grow up in the same place and never have to move, but change can also be a positive.

When you move, your children can be better for it. As I was moving as a child and then moving with my children as an adult, my motto was "Wherever I am planted, I will bloom in that spot." I always got involved, and I taught my children to do the same thing. My message to my children was this: *Get involved where you are; make new friends where you are. Do not just sit back and say, "Well, I did not want to move here, so I am not going to get involved. I am unhappy here; I will not find new friends, and I will just be sad and angry about it."*

Your children must learn to bloom where they are planted because that is the way they will find happiness. Allow them and encourage them to take advantage of the opportunities that the new place will bring them. They will learn about new opportunities that maybe they would not have had before.

When you have to make those changes to improve your family life or those changes come without choice, embrace them. If you help and support your children to work through the change, they will be okay. The change will likely be a character-building experience that will empower them and give them new confidence.

Character Building

Every time your children face problems, every time they accept change and work through change, they grow in character—every single time. Realize that what is difficult for your children will not kill them. Raise your children to accept that they will face difficulties in life but that they will be able to work through them. Adversity and challenge will require determination and grit, but they will be stronger because of the effort they put into working through challenges.

Raise empowered children. Help your children see that every time they overcome a challenge, they are stronger because of it. As they face changes in life, they are growing, learning, and experiencing. Each and every change will provide an opportunity for growth and empowerment if they work their way through it.

When my youngest daughter came to the realization that she was engaged too young and was not ready to get married, she wanted to talk through that decision with me. She said that she was afraid others would judge her if she called off the engagement. I told her, "You have to do what is right for you. No one is going to judge you for being mature enough to realize that you are not ready to get married at this point in your life. It is better to make that decision now than to go through with the wedding, realizing from the start that you are really too young to be married. Better to end an engagement than a marriage."

We had raised her, just like our other children, to face difficult situations and to make those difficult decisions. As scared as she was about what people were going to think of her and as heartbreaking as it was to tell her fiancé, she made the difficult decision to end the engagement. She had learned to make difficult decisions because she had faced problems, changes, and challenges before. She knew she could survive the consequences of the difficult decision because this had been built into her character.

When your children are empowered, they realize how strong they are. They will know with certainty that they can work through challenges and do what is in their own best interest. Give your children the gift of facing problems and accepting change so that they can embrace life with the confidence needed to make the best decisions for themselves even when they know the decisions they have to make are difficult ones.

Epilogue

Motherhood is not a hobby, it is a calling. It is not something to do if you can squeeze the time in. It is what God gave you time for.
—Neil L. Anderson

Throughout this book, we have talked about gifts that you can give your children. I hope that every single gift is something that you will think about, expand on, and implement within your own family with your own children.

As moms, you have the power to change the world, and you *are* changing the world, one child at a time. None of us can know what our children are going to become as adults; we do not know what kind of people they will be. All we know is that we must raise them the best that we can and instill in them the values that we feel are vital to a purposeful life.

Recognize how powerful your role is. You are a mom; treasure it. Do not let anything else get in the way of being Mom. No matter what your job is, whether you have a career outside the home or whether you are a stay-at-home mom, whatever you do, recognize that being a mom is your number one priority. Raising happy, positive, responsible, empowered, and kind people is the greatest accomplishment you will ever have. Be the mom your children truly need, and create the family you always wanted. Give your children the twelve greatest gifts.

61319579R00144

Made in the USA
Lexington, KY
09 March 2017